45 935 888 I

D1577275

SOBERS
The Changing Face
of Cricket

SOBERS

The Changing Face of Cricket

Sir Garfield Sobers

WITH IVO TENNANT

EBURY PRESS

First published in 1996 by Ebury Press
1 3 5 7 9 10 8 6 4 2

Ebury Press
Random House, 20 Vauxhall Bridge Road,
London SW1V 2SA

Random House Australia (Pty) Limited
20 Alfred Street, Milsons Point, Sydney
New South Wales 2061, Australia

Random House New Zealand Limited
18 Poland Road, Glenfield
Auckland 10, New Zealand

Random House South Africa (Pty) Limited
PO Box 2263, Rosebank 2121, South Africa

Random House UK Limited Reg. No. 954009

A CIP catalogue record for this book
is available from the British Library

ISBN: 0 09 180713 1

Edited by Alison Wormleighton
Designed by Roger Walker

Printed and bound in Great Britain by
Butler and Tanner Ltd, Frome, Somerset

Papers used by Ebury Press are natural, recyclable products
made from wood grown in sustainable forests.

ACKNOWLEDGEMENTS

The publishers would like to thank the following for permission to
reproduce the photographs used in this book: Colour plates: All
Sport (plates 9, 10, 11, 12, 13, 14); Patrick Eager (plates 1, 2, 3, 4,
5, 6, 7, 8). Black-and-white photographs: All Sport (p 3); Associated
Press (p 63); Barbados News (pp 5, 33); Brooks La Touche (pp 10,
26, 148); Central Press (pp 16, 82,93); CPNE (p 160 – bottom);
Graham Morris (pp 81, 131, 132); London Photo Agency (p 160 –
top); Press Association (p 42); Reuter (pp 57, 59); Sport & General
(pp 19, 29, 138); Thomson Newspapers (pp 105, 113, 146, 177);
Times Newspapers (pp 39, 49); United Press International (p 77).

Contents

Foreword

Sir Garfield Sobers enjoys the unique distinction of being universally acknowledged as the most complete cricketer the game has ever known.

Sir Gary, as he is known throughout the cricketing world, was recognized as a potential genius from his early days when representing Barbados at the tender age of 16. After one year in first class cricket, he was in the West Indies team and immediately made his presence felt.

I recall being padded up to bat at number three against Australia in Barbados in 1955, when Sir Gary opened the innings. In the first over from Keith Miller, the great Australian all-rounder, Sir Gary crashed four fours and scored 40 of his 43 runs in boundaries. This was all to the delight of his home crowd.

It was not until 1958 that he scored his first Test century, which resulted in a world record 365 Not Out against Pakistan at Sabina Park, Jamaica.

I had the pleasure of batting with Sir Gary when he reached that record score, and what a great occasion it was. But, of course, this record was comprehensively broken by star batsman Brian Lara in Antigua in 1994. Indeed, Sir Gary was delighted to witness this magnificent feat. Typically, he was one of the first rushing onto the field to congratulate Brian.

To highlight all of his outstanding achievements with bat and ball and his many brilliant catches would take volumes. I will, however, repeat a few accolades from outstanding world personalities.

Sir Donald Bradman, who saw him score 254 for a World XI against Australia in Melbourne in 1971–72 said, "It was certainly the best innings I have ever seen on Australian soil." Sir Gary is remembered not only for his remarkable trail of statistical records, but for the quality of his cricket and the way he enjoyed the game.

The eminent cricket writer E W Swanton reminds us that "the true measure of his influence must take account of his sportsmanship and an unselfishness that were never questioned, an example second to none".

On the more philosophical plane, C L R James remarked, "A man of genius is what he is, he cannot be something else and remain a man of genius."

Any one of Sir Gary's three styles of bowling would have earned him a place in any Test team, but his fast medium swing bowling, particularly with the new ball, was feared by most batsmen. His brilliant close-to-the wicket catching made him the complete cricketer and undoubtedly the best all-round cricketer to have played the game.

Sir Gary retired from the game in 1974 and one year later was knighted by the Queen in recognition of his outstanding contribution to world cricket – a fitting honour to this cricketing genius.

Since Sir Gary's retirement, cricket has been an ever-changing scene. The one-day limited-overs game with its white balls and brightly coloured outfits, not to mention day/night matches made possible by floodlights, is here to stay. The one-day game has captured the imagination of a huge new cricket following due mainly to the media, be it newspaper coverage or in more recent years the television, bringing every detail of the game into the home.

Even the appearance of the cricketer on the field has undergone change – the helmets, the elbow, chest and shin guards, and more recently the dark shades.

The game has also become more professional and commercialized and, as a result, more competitive, leading to the creation of new rules and regulations. Two of the most topical changes are the limitation of fast, short-pitched bowling and the number of overs to be bowled in a day's play. It has been said that if fast, short-pitched balls were limited in Sir Gary's playing days, he might have made fewer runs, as he played that type of bowling really well.

In recent times there have been growing concerns about declining standards of behaviour and this has prompted the International Cricket Council to introduce a Code of Conduct to provide uniform and fair control of players' behaviour through the appointment of independent match referees. These referees are intended to provide vital support to the umpires.

As a follow-up to match referees, there is an international panel of umpires from which one is chosen to officiate at each Test match. There is also a third umpire who, with the use of a television monitor, gives decisions on run-outs, stumpings and hit wickets when called upon by the officiating umpires.

I can think of no better person than Gary to comment on how he sees the game with its many changes and I am confident that his views will be widely read by all cricket enthusiasts, particularly the contemporary generation of players who all regard him as cricket's consummate star.

Sir Clyde Walcott, KA, OBE, AA

CHAPTER 1

Calypso Connection

Virtually everything that needed to be written about my life in cricket has already been written. Indeed, everything that needed to be written about my life *off* the field during my 20 years in active cricket is also already on record. This book, *Sobers: The Changing Face of Cricket*, looks beyond my years as an active player during two decades, 1954–1974.

The books on my years as an active player have become part of the literature of a game whose history has been more carefully and extensively documented than has been the case in any other game. Cricket and cricketers have inspired some of the best literature ever written on any sport, none more so than the seminal work of the West Indian intellectual, C R L James, *Beyond a Boundary*, considered by many to be the best book ever written on cricket. I commend James's words to all cricketers everywhere: "What do they know of cricket, who only cricket know?" It is both a challenge and an opportunity to hold up a mirror and look at oneself and look into the heartland of the game.

In addition, I often say that no other game has taken its heroes and their achievements and celebrated them so magnificently in song. For West Indians, with a strong oral tradition rooted in their predominantly African heritage, this is not surprising and it has brought all West Indies players great joy

1

when playing both at home and abroad. In my day a stack of records was as normal a part of one's travelling equipment as pads or gloves. Today the team never leaves home without a good supply of cassette tapes and CDs. And of course every team produces a balladeer or calypsonian. We had Seymour Nurse. Today Curtly Ambrose is the travelling calypsonian.

Calypso, the unique music of the Caribbean, has been used with exquisite skill by Caribbean singers to celebrate the successes and failures of West Indian cricket through the years, from Lord Beginner's "Those two little pals of mine, Ramadhin and Valentine" in 1950 to the songs celebrating the magnificent achievements of Brian Lara in 1994.

At the same time, cricket writers looking for an apt description of the flamboyant style and natural rhythm of West Indian cricketers christened us "calypso cricketers". That was before we became champions of world cricket and demonstrated the ability not only to play the game attractively but also to remain at the top for 15 years, refusing to surrender our sovereignty and bringing pride and joy to our people.

My own achievements have attracted the attention of the calypsonians and I could not help noticing the presence of some of the region's top singers at the Antigua Recreation Ground when Lara broke my record on 18 April 1994. The same was true at Queen's Park Oval in the same series on the final morning of the third Test match after Ambrose had left England teetering on the brink of ignominious defeat at 44 for 8. They came, guitars in hand, to celebrate history in song, capturing the feelings of victors and vanquished alike in a truly West Indian idiom.

"Cricket, Lovely Cricket"

It is encouraging that academics are turning their attention to documenting many facets of the game. Some day, some enthusiastic student of the game will document for posterity

BEACH CRICKET IS AN INTEGRAL PART OF LIFE IN THE CARIBBEAN

the number of calypsos which have been written about cricket and its heroes. I can think of no words that capture the spirit of any other game better than the memorable verses of Lord Beginner in his 1950 calypso "Cricket, Lovely Cricket, at Lord's where I saw it".

That song marked a sea change both for cricket and for calypso as an art form. Just as calypso was indigenous to the West Indies, so, too, West Indian cricketers would take an English game and put their own peculiar stamp on it with skills developed on rough tracts in the islands. I often say that in assessing the march of progress in West Indian cricket, it is important to note that we conquered poverty and deprivation by putting to use our own ingenuity, developing makeshift bats rough-hewn from a variety of tropical trees and balls from indigenous materials freely available in all of the islands. Not only did we play the game our way, we also played it from an early age with our own home-made equipment. And that, believe me, made it all the sweeter.

The greatest thing about the game when I played was the high level of camaraderie and the genuine friendships made which survive even today. Cricket changed my life. The small island where I was born, Barbados, which is 21 miles long and 14 miles wide with a population of 250,000, has consistently produced more world-class cricketers per square mile than any other country. Playing cricket gave me an opportunity to meet on and off the field people from different countries, cultures, religions, and ethnic groups as well as all social classes. They were not all cricketers, but to me, they were all worthy human beings and I respected them all as such.

Communication is as important in cricket on and off the field as it is in any other aspect of life. On one of my early visits to England I read the views of a university professor who claimed that the ability to communicate verbally was the basic characteristic separating mankind and the animals. Such an ability – to communicate easily both on and off the field and to

WHERE IT ALL BEGAN. SIR GARY'S CHILDHOOD HOME IN BAY LAND,
NEAR BRIDGETOWN

move easily and comfortably among all sorts of people everywhere – has served me well throughout my life.

Cricket not only changed my life, it proved to be the best
way of learning about life. Though I was from a small country,
the whole cricketing world was my playing field. Cricket
broadened my outlook for the better and made me, as nothing
else could have, a citizen of the world. That some consider me
a gentleman who played the game in the spirit which made it
a noble sport is an added bonus.

There were great pioneers in West Indies cricket before me
who did a fantastic job in bringing attention and prestige to
the West Indies – players like Headley, Constantine, Weekes,
Worrell and Walcott, Ramadhin and Valentine. They were
men who by the sheer brilliance of their skills took an English
game and honed it into a West Indian art to the delight of
people across the globe. Even in retirement, as I reflect on my
playing days I find it difficult to assess my impact on the game.
Perhaps it is best that I let my record speak for me since the
cold, hard statistical facts can be judged for themselves.

The spirit of the game

There are three things that I know for sure. The first is that I
always put my team and the public above all else. Cricket is a
team sport and I was always one of eleven men. Whether I was
playing for the West Indies or Barbados, county cricket in England or in the Sheffield Shield in Australia, a one-day match or
a Test match, I always made my own interests secondary to that
of the team. Players must use their ability to promote the collective interests of the team above their individual interests.

Secondly, I always saw cricket as a noble sport and I tried to
play in the true spirit of the game. Hence, I seldom if ever lost
my cool and I never questioned the umpire's decision. At all
times, whether I was playing on a cold, bleak Saturday evening
in a mundane Lancashire League match on a green-top wicket

or playing at Lord's, Sydney or Kensington Oval on a bright, sunny morning, I always enjoyed my game and always tried to make sure that those watching me also enjoyed whatever I was doing.

Thirdly, like the greatest captain the game was privileged to see in my playing days, Sir Frank Worrell, I always believed that a captain must lead by example. A true leader cannot be like the Duke of Parma and command his troops from behind. I believed in being in the vanguard of the battle, taking the new ball from the established opening bowlers when the task ahead looked daunting and taking the fight to the opposition. I relished moving in to what commentators called "suicidal positions" close to the bat to put added pressure on a new batsman or one with a well-known dislike of the short-pitched ball. When we were batting and the opposing bowlers were less than menacing, I was always prepared to slip down the order and give a batsman struggling to find his form a chance to play a confidence-boosting innings.

During the two decades since my retirement the game has undergone fundamental changes. Those changes have gone unnoticed by the singers and will never be part of the rich literature of the game. In this book I wish to reflect on those changes and share my thoughts with lovers of the game.

Cricket has already shown its ability to adapt to changing times and turn to its best advantage new challenges facing the game and cricketers across the globe. Only by accepting that change is both necessary and beneficial can all those involved in cricket reap the full benefits while preserving those fundamental traditions which make cricket for me the greatest game known to mankind.

CHAPTER 2

In the Wake of Retirement

In 1994, to celebrate the 40th anniversary of my Test debut, the Government of Barbados in conjunction with a number of other bodies organized a series of commemorative events. One such event was a series of lectures by eminent Caribbean citizens. These were published in a book, *An Area of Conquest: Popular Democracy and West Indies Cricket Supremacy*, in November 1994, and contributed significantly to the literature on the game. I will always treasure the many fine tributes paid to me during the commemorative year and appreciate the efforts of the organizing committee chaired by my friend and former playing colleague, Rawle Brancker. My Prime Minister's tribute, however, was one of the finest and this I shall always treasure highly. The text of his speech at the launch of the book is given at the end of this book.

The committee did a marvellous job in organizing the series of celebratory events. Many people worked long and hard to ensure their success, none more so than my dear friend and former Minister of Sport in Barbados, Wes Hall. Wes and I have enjoyed a close personal and professional friendship for over 40 years and no one knows me better.

It was the first time that there were so many dedicated events to celebrate the achievements of any Barbadian or West Indian player or, indeed, any player from any country. The celebrations were not restricted to my native Barbados – one that I will never forget took place in Toronto, Canada. It was attended by almost 1000 people and chaired by Clive Lloyd, who flew across four continents to be there.

The whole idea for the celebratory year was the brainchild of Tony Arthur, the acting Director of the Barbados Tourist Board at the time. His idea was discussed with the then Prime Minister Erskine Sandiford, who gave it his blessing. A year later, while on a promotional tour in Australia, Wes Hall revived the idea.

As I did not earn a great deal from the game, the celebratory events amounted to a Benefit. Trustees, chaired by an old friend, Philip Greaves, and including Peter Short and David Simmons, the Attorney General in Barbados, were appointed to administer the funds raised, which at the time of writing amount to $300,000 (Barbados dollars, or £100,000). It was Philip Greaves' idea for this money, currently in a fixed deposit account, to be put into a trust fund which will effectively be my pension. I shall not forget the generosity of the Bajan people, nor their acclaim when I was helicoptered in to the same spot on the Garrison Savannah where the Queen had knighted me nearly two decades before.

That memorable outdoor ceremony in 1975, when I was knighted by Queen Elizabeth II with 25,000 spectators looking on, was undoubtedly the most significant award I have received in my life. Second to that I rank the conferring of an Honorary Doctorate of Laws by the University of the West Indies at the Barbados campus in 1992. The words of the citation I received on that occasion are given at the end of this book.

Unaccustomed injury

If I have one regret about the programme of activities for the 40th anniversary celebrations, it was that because of physical disabilities caused by eye and knee problems, I could not

KNIGHTED BY THE QUEEN AT THE SAVANNAH, BARBADOS, IN 1975

actually make an appearance on the field and do what I have always enjoyed doing most and what has brought me to the attention of the world. It is ironic that having played all forms of cricket continuously for 20 years without suffering any major physical injury, after retiring from the game I suffered two major injuries in two years, both of which landed me in hospital to undergo surgery.

I made my debut for the West Indies at Sabina Park in 1954, the year after my debut for Barbados. During the next 18 years I never had any problems and never missed a match until I pulled a muscle in the 1971/72 Rest of the World series. The record will show that I played 87 consecutive Test matches for the West Indies, never missing any through injury and establishing a world record for the number of Test matches played sequentially. As one commentator has also noted, I seldom, if ever, left the field for any reason. But life plays strange tricks on all of us.

In December 1992 I had to be rushed to Miami for an emergency operation for a detached and torn retina. To this day I cannot explain how it got detached. I just recall having a dark spot in my left eye and after seeing specialists in Jamaica, having to undergo emergency surgery on what the surgeon said was the worst case he had seen for a long time. I was given only a 50/50 chance of regaining my sight in the eye.

The operation was a success and the surgeon and I shared the happy news. Soon afterwards, however, I developed post-operative complications and had to have further corrective surgery. In all, I spent a month in Miami during which two of my former colleagues, Lance Gibbs and Jackie Hendriks, showered me in warm, caring hospitality. I lost partial vision in the eye and have reconciled myself to the reality that it will not come back.

Still, I am none the worse for what was a frightening experience, although my golf has been affected and my vision is sometimes impaired on the golf course, especially when playing bunker shots. I give thanks daily to God, my surgeons, family and legion of friends, acquaintances and fans from across the globe who stood by me in those dark days. Cricket was a marvellous way of making friends across the world who in good times and bad have given me their support.

The second crisis

My second medical crisis occurred in 1993, 31 years after recurring pain in my left knee had forced me to have a minor operation for a knee injury. I had carried that injury for a while. I had asked Sir Reginald Watson-Jones, the orthopedic surgeon at London University Hospital, to perform the operation. It was a success and I went back to Australia and did the double of 50 wickets and 1000 runs, helping South Australia to become runners-up in the Sheffield Shield.

Just before the Australian tour of West Indies in 1972 I was beginning to experience increasing pain in the same knee and my movement was being increasingly impaired. The surgeon discovered that there had been major deterioration, to the extent that he was surprised that I was still able to play cricket at the highest level almost all year round. His diagnosis was that the bones were rubbing against each other and the friction created caused them to flake away.

The doctors advised me that the only solution was the removal of the cartilage. Throughout my life I have never argued with highly qualified professionals. I had the operation, which was successful. I went 20 years without any major problems with my knees until early in 1993, when I started feeling pain in my right knee to the point where my golf game was suffering significantly. A visit to my surgeon confirmed my worst fears – I would have to get a replacement joint.

By now the pain in my knee had became quite excruciating and I had no logical choice but to follow the surgeon's advice. I went into hospital in Barbados, had laser surgery, was discharged the same day and was walking and generally feeling a whole lot better. The next day I walked back into the hospital to let the surgeon have a quick look. He was as happy as I was. I felt so good that two days after the operation I played nine holes of golf using an electric cart. Two days later I played a full 18 holes at Sandy Lane with no after-effects. I marvelled at the advances that modern medicine could deliver to weary, old joints. My friends marvelled that I was walking again like the Sobers of old.

My job as a sports consultant with the Barbados Tourism Authority took me soon afterwards to the World Travel Market in London. Within days of arriving in England, the knee was swollen and painful. My first thoughts were that the healing process had been compromised by excessive standing and walking after my arrival in London. I took a long soak in a hot bathtub that night and went to bed. Next morning the knee was worse and to my horror I discovered that I could not walk. In addition to the physical disability, the psychological impact of not being able to walk was devastating.

I knew that I was in serious trouble. The hotel doctor was called, had a look and recommended antibiotics. That was on the Saturday and I had a most uncomfortable Sunday. Worse still, I was scheduled to leave on the Monday to return to Barbados. Encouraged by the same doctor, early on the Monday morning I agreed that a specialist should be called in. His response was immediate and frightening. "Sir Gary," he said, "I am going to have you admitted to hospital immediately. I don't like the look of this knee one little bit. We need to take a closer clinical look without further delay."

I was taken to the hospital within a matter of hours. I was in pain and very down in the dumps. The surgeon told me that he would have to drain the fluid off the knee. The sight of the needle sent shivers down my spine. As he drew off a sample of fluid, the doctor looked at me with a half smile on his face and said, "Sir Gary, if you were planning to return to

13

Barbados anytime soon, I have news for you. You will not be going anywhere for a long time. I am afraid you will have to be here for a little while yet." That was at six o'clock. At nine o'clock that night I went into the surgery to have the inflammation which had built up in the knee removed. Two days later I had to return to the surgery. The doctor's calm words will haunt me until I die. "Sir Gary," he said, "You are a very sick lad indeed." In all, I spent almost a month in hospital including being on a drip for almost a week. Every time I saw the surgeon I had a standard question: "Doc, have I got to go back into the surgery again?" Just being laid up in bed was bad enough, but the very thought of more surgery was frightening.

In the event, further surgery was not necessary. The knee healed nicely after I returned home and stuck vigorously to the recommended medication. For the next three months I walked with the aid of crutches. To see me – who in my heyday was considered the supreme athlete – reduced to hobbling and wearing dark glasses, was guaranteed to bring quizzical smiles to the faces of my friends. For me it was a sobering reminder of how frail the human body is. It has been tough on me, but I have made the necessary adjustments, which is what life and getting old are all about – adjusting to change.

It has never been easy for me to accept the praise and adulation which have been heaped upon me through the years, though I might have appeared calm in everything I did on the field in my playing days. There were many times, however, during the tributes of 1994 when I was quietly tearful, none more so than at the grand banquet held at the magnificent new gymnasium named in my honour when my two sons joined me on the stage.

Great kids

Let me say a few words about my sons, Matthew and Daniel, who are very close to me and of whom I am particularly proud.

They are kids of whom any parent would feel justifiably proud. They are not just fine children, but lots of fun to have around. In a very real sense we dote on each other and spend a lot of time together whenever my very hectic travelling schedule permits. Matthew graduated from the University of the West Indies in 1993 with a Bachelor of Science degree in Accountancy and is now a hotel management trainee. Danny is a graphic artist. Whereas Matthew has been my constant companion since the break-up of my marriage, Danny has spent more time in Australia with his mother.

One of the things I am constantly asked wherever I go is why my boys have not played the game with any distinction. They have both tried it, with varying degrees of success, but have really developed their own sporting interests quite independently. As a father, I have never been the one to insist that they play cricket or any particular game. I would rather give them full rein to follow their own instincts and interests. I have always subscribed to the view that children should enjoy full freedom to pursue their own interests and careers without having a domineering parent making the choices. Guidance by all means, but the final choice must be the child's.

Matthew has played Australian Rules Football and now plays basketball, volleyball, soccer, table tennis, badminton and dominoes. With a heavy workload since graduation, his leisure activities are now severely restricted. Danny prefers water sports. He swims well and is devoted to surfing. He spends much of his spare time pursuing both in Barbados and Australia, where he returned late last year to further his interest in graphic arts.

No father could have asked for better kids and we are more like brothers than is the case in the usual father/son relationship. A large part of the very strong sense of mutual affection and love we share has its roots in the fact that, since my ex-wife Pru returned to Australia, I became a father who mothered them in their adolescent years, and the bonding is deep and

A NEW MEMBER OF THE TEAM. HOLDING MATTHEW ALOFT IN
MELBOURNE IN 1971

enduring. I greatly regretted, however, that my daughter, Genevieve, who is now 16 and lives with her mother in Australia, could not join her brothers and myself in Barbados for the celebrations. Yet the boys and I knew that she was very much with us in spirit. She, too, is a great kid and I feel blessed that the Sobers name, if not the cricketing tradition, will be carried forward to the next generation by my children.

My life now

I hardly needed to do or think about anything other than cricket from the age of 17 or 18 until I retired. From time to time as I neared the end of my career, an interviewer would ask me what I intended to do when I retired from the game. I would reply that something along the lines of working in the government service in the West Indies would suit me. England was too cold in the winter (and sometimes in the summer!) to contemplate living there all the year round and Australia was too far from home, although I did come to live there for a while after marrying an Australian. I stressed, though, that I could not sit behind a desk for long. I have always wanted to express myself in the way I attempted to do on the cricket field. I would have liked to have found a young cricketer in the backstreets of Bridgetown who would have emulated my cricketing achievements. In a strange, rather selfish way, I would have liked to have been the person to introduce him to other Bajans.

I was 38 when I retired. I could have continued playing first-class cricket until I was 40, or perhaps even longer, but the amount of travelling and living out of a suitcase that I was still undertaking was beginning to take its toll. I had suffered knee injuries and felt the more gentle pull of the golf course. In all probability, I had made more money out of the game than anybody else at that time, but my future was far from secure. It was no secret that before I married in 1969, I had led a full social life and enjoyed the horses. But I was disappointed by a great deal of the financial advice and so-called guidance I had been given. I became more wary, even cynical, about people coming up to me and offering this kind of service.

I was employed, initially, by CARICOM, the federation of Caribbean nations, before moving from Nottingham to Melbourne once World Series Cricket started. I was fond of Australians, and to my wife, Prue, Melbourne was home. She wished to remain there after my work for Kerry Packer finished, as she had her own career as a writer and did not want to move to Barbados, where I had always wanted to return eventually. My mother was still alive and I had too many ties to take me away for long. I fear Prue had had enough of my travelling, so I went home to the Caribbean and took a job with the Barbados Board of Tourism. Later on, my old friend and colleague Wes Hall became a Senator and the Minister for Tourism and Sport.

I have no ambitions remaining within cricket and do not have the aptitude to be an administrator or the patience to be a selector, umpire or team manager. However, my work for the Board of Tourism does allow me sufficient spare time to help clubs through the Barbados Cricket Association. I like to talk to young players about attitude, concentration, mental approach and technical aspects that might make a difference of 40 runs to a batsman or two to three wickets for a bowler.

I have worked now for the Board, which is based in Bridgetown, since 1980 and want to continue doing so, to encourage visitors to come to Barbados. I am not a great one for public speaking but am quite willing to speak to enthusiasts at schools, clubs and so on. I don't feel there is a danger of too much tourism or of the south coast, where many of the hotels are clustered, becoming too built up. The great beauty of the island is not being spoiled.

There was some criticism of the English supporters who watched the Test in Barbados in 1994 and who became very vociferous through too much drink and too much sun. But I

18

HELPING MAKE A FILM FOR THE CHILDREN'S FILM
FOUNDATION IN 1970

don't think a certain amount of exuberance does any harm. They brought much-needed finance with them and that, ultimately, is what Barbados is dependent on. I don't think we have to be afraid of the football hooligan type and, if they do come, we can remove them. Visitors come up to me in the street or at the ground and say, "You're lucky with what you've got here." We have had the occasional storm, but nothing serious. There has been some crime, as there has everywhere else, and although it is not easy to stamp out, we've always been able to curb it. We suffered like all other islands during the recession but when the economy picked up, so, too, did tourism.

Our marketing strategy has looked up. An excellent conference centre has been built near the Prime Minister's residence. We have a wide range of hotels and opportunities for all sportsmen, the gymnasium named after me and a jazz festival. The Board is trying to attract incentive groups: if employees of a firm work hard, then they are given an incentive holiday.

I work for the Board on a consultancy basis, which means I travel a considerable amount, particularly to London, and am involved in entertaining visitors and potential visitors to Barbados. Then there are numerous speaking engagements and appearances on television and on radio in addition to the small amount of commentating on the game that I do. Quite often my work for the Board, which is effectively public relations, takes me to countries where there is a Test match in progress. Then I can combine work and pleasure.

CHAPTER 3

Young Players and Youth Cricket

England and Australia have always taught the basics well to young cricketers, notably at indoor cricket schools such as Alf Gover's and Middlesex County Cricket School. However, during my time and perhaps before, West Indians tended to pick up the finer points of the game by watching players of the class of George Headley and the three "W's" (Walcott, Weekes and Worrell). Grammar schools in the Caribbean did provide some coaching, but this would not account for the success of players such as Everton Weekes, Seymour Nurse and myself. Once we had established ourselves, and players of the calibre of Everton and Seymour had become coaches, many more Bajan boys were able to benefit, but by today's standards even that would be inadequate.

Waiting too long

The Indians and Pakistanis have always brought their best young players into their teams at an early age. Trawl through the list of cricketers showing the ages at which they made their debuts and you will see that nine of the youngest ten are from the sub-continent. Mushtaq Mohammad was only 15 when he played against West Indies in 1958–59. I have always felt, as one who was the second youngest West Indian to make his debut – I was 17 years and 245 days old when I made my debut, against England at Sabina Park in 1953–54 – that too often other countries, including West Indies, wait too long to bring their promising young players, batsmen in particular, into their Test teams.

Take Brian Lara: he should have been brought into the West Indies team about two years earlier, especially when there were players in the side who were failing consistently, had not achieved their early potential and clearly had no future. Yet the selectors persisted with them. Brian was 22 when he came to England on the 1991 tour but did not appear in any of the Tests in that series. It is interesting to note that whereas selectors appear ready to give a fast bowler a try at an early age, they seem to expect a promising batsman to wait much longer. During the '70s and '80s there always appeared to be a place available to any promising young player who possessed pace. This worked marvellously well when Wes Hall, Charlie Griffith and, more recently, Curtly Ambrose and Ian Bishop were young.

The same was not true of spinners. Rhajindra Dhanrajh, who showed great potential early in his career, had to wait much too long before he was given a place in the West Indies team. As a schoolboy player he was as good a bowler as Lara was a batsman. Yet when we look at the way their careers have gone, we must ask whether, had there had not been such a heavy emphasis on a four-prong fast attack, he too would not have become a West Indian star. In the few Tests he has been given, he has struggled to make an impression, not least in England in 1995.

One of the most significant developments in the changing face of the game has been the growth of youth cricket. This has given young cricketers the opportunity of playing against their peers in various conditions, in different parts of the world and in diverse cultural settings. Hence there are opportunities to develop not only excellent players but also excellent, well-rounded young men. Under-19 "Tests" are an ideal way of enabling teenagers to have a taste of international cricket and of touring.

When I started playing first-class cricket in Barbados, at the age of 15, I had to play against established players who had made a name for themselves at Test level like John Goddard, Everton Weekes and Clyde Walcott. These days the young players get more exposure by playing among themselves in the youth series, going from the national youth teams into the West Indies youth team. This is a good breeding ground and has produced Malcolm Marshall, Jeff Dujon, Roland Holder, Jimmy Adams, Lara, Shivnarine Chanderpaul, Carl Hooper, Roger Harper and Sherwin Campbell. Playing in different conditions away from home has been of great benefit to young players in all countries. It equips them when they make the Test side to adapt to conditions which would have been totally strange and difficult if they had not been exposed to them before. How I wish that I had had the experience of playing on a green-top in England as a young player. I am also sure that there are many English players who would have benefited greatly from playing on hard, fast, true wickets like those in the West Indies and Australia.

International youth tournament

One of the developments in youth cricket of which I feel very proud has been the outstanding success of the Sir Garfield Sobers youth tournament. What started in 1987 as a very limited series of matches has now blossomed into a truly international series. Since then, teams have come from Canada, Dominica, England, Grenada, Jamaica, Scotland, South Africa, St Vincent, Trinidad & Tobago and host country Barbados. The tournament was originally the idea of a Bajan tour operator, Don Gooding. His aim was to encourage schools from England to visit Barbados off season – in other words, in the English summer months.

Several youth tournament players have gone on to represent their countries and many others are on the threshold of international recognition. To me, the single most significant feature of this cricket has been the spirit of camaraderie and warm fellowship in which the game is always played and the friendships which have grown among the numerous young men of many nations. That, above all else, is the essence of cricket both at youth and more mature levels.

The tournament, which is run in conjunction with the Barbados Sports Council, has been fortunate to attract sponsorship from Barbados and Sabona of London. My role is to try to help raise this, which is not easy. I also go around the grounds and hotels, talking to the parents, boys and masters. Tourism is the beneficiary from the tournament through the presence on the island of a number of parents who accompany the youngsters, and the tournament is now a significant addition to the sports tourism calendar. In talking to the young players on tour, it is obvious that one of the things they look forward to most is meeting and talking with former great West Indian players who live in Barbados – Sir Clyde Walcott, Wes Hall, Everton Weekes, Charlie Griffith, Seymour Nurse, Gordon Greenidge, Desmond Haynes, David Holford and Joel "Big Bird" Garner.

These former players are always ready to share their experiences and knowledge with the youths and accompany them from ground to ground. This is great for the morale of the youngsters, who are flattered to see cricket greats taking time off from their busy schedules to watch them play. One incentive to do well in the tournament is the possibility of participating in the play-off final at Kensington Oval, one of the most famous cricket grounds in the world, in the presence of some of the game's best-known personalities.

For the tenth anniversary in 1996, 20 schools are taking part, more than ever before. One English school has been to the tournament four times and quite a few others have returned on two or three occasions, but none has won. The first school outside the Caribbean to win the tournament was from South Africa, which is an indication of the talent that will be coming through in that country. I am pleased with the standard. The boys play nine to 11 games in three weeks, so I can understand why they want to spend their days off on the beach, not in team meetings.

Cricket academies

I think that a cricket academy is important to the future development of West Indian cricket and I would like to see one properly established utilizing the best available ex-players as coaches. As the game becomes more lucrative and playing schedules more demanding, it is going to be imperative that all cricketing nations develop cricket academies to hone the raw skills of their players under expert guidance. The one in Australia has been a marvellous development.

In the West Indies, there has been a considerable amount of talk about initiating an academy, possibly one specializing in different aspects of the game in different islands. In other words, batting could be taught in Barbados, fast bowling in Jamaica, slow bowling in Trinidad and so on. This would be rather like the University of the West Indies, with different campuses installed all round the region.

Coaching

I believe that the right tutor will be of help to a young player, but I have to be frank and admit that I do not believe in too much coaching! We live in an era in which the coach is considered to be of paramount importance, if not a sacrosanct individual, but there are a lot of people involved in coaching who do not fully understand how to do it. Moreover, many wish to be associated with the talented player likely to make a

DEMONSTRATING THE CORRECT TECHNIQUE TO THE NEXT
GENERATION IN BARBADOS

name for himself rather than trying to develop the ability of the player of lesser talent.

And all too many coaches favour mass production, tutoring from the MCC manual or another handbook. They will say: "Don't play that shot – it's a bad shot." Instead of taking away from a batsman his natural inclinations, a coach should be able to work on them. A batsman's natural flair is gone if that particular shot is taken away from him. But the coach's reputation then suffers if he has different ideas to the rest because he does not have the same robotic approach.

I think that too much emphasis is placed on the academic qualifications of having a coaching certification. I worked with a number of players who had coaching certificates and yet they knew nothing. They had read books and passed exams but when it came to the nitty-gritty they knew nothing about the game. The idea, prevalent since my playing days, that qualifications are all-important in so many areas of life, is flawed. I know a registrar in Guyana, a man who never gained a degree, who was one of the best they ever had there. Intuition, as much as technical knowledge, makes a good cricket coach. The success, for instance, of Bob Woolmer first with Warwickshire and then with South Africa amazes me because when I played against him I never felt he had that aptitude. Clearly, though, he possesses a great enthusiasm, a love for the game, which is the first criterion.

By the same token, not every good cricketer will make a good coach. Communication techniques and inter-personal skills are essential for this. The coach must always be able to point out what a player is doing wrong, why he is doing it wrong, the effect of doing it wrong and how to correct the fault and bring about some benefit.

There is a danger that cricket coaching can become like a lesson at school: do this, don't do that. Coaching is tedious and is about trying to hold the pupils' interest and getting the message over in the least complicated way. A boy should not think

27

that he is being taught cricket but that he is participating in something fun. I have not changed my long-held view that there should be a few diversions to constant coaching. Football, volleyball, skipping and baseball can help the coordination of both the average cricketer and the first-class player. A steady head and quick feet are the fundamental requirements for cricket, and that is increasingly the case in an era of fast bowling. Until those fundamentals are mastered, there is no purpose in delving into technicalities.

Permanent coaches

I was delighted when the West Indian cricket administrators took a significant step forward in appointing Rohan Kanhai as coach of the West Indies team. He fully deserved the position, having been coach of the Jamaica youth team as well as Jamaica itself. He did an excellent job, operating precisely as a good coach should – helping the captain with the technical aspects of the game as they relate to his own team and spotting the weaknesses and flaws of the opposition.

Rohan was the first proper coach the West Indies employed. He has now returned to coaching in Jamaica, for the policy in the Caribbean is to give the job, as with the post of manager, to different people in turn. I would like to think that in every cricket-playing country the administrations will appoint coaches to perform the functions Rohan has carried out for the West Indies and Bobby Simpson has undertaken for Australia. England now prefer to use specialist coaches rather than one permanent employee in Keith Fletcher and this baffles me. I recall, for example, when Geoff Arnold came out to the Caribbean at one stage to handle only the fast bowlers. I firmly believe that one coach should look after all aspects of the game, otherwise there are too many people going around with the team. Soon the situation will arise whereby there is a specialist fielding coach.

UNCOACHED BUT ALWAYS ORTHODOX. SWINGING JOHN PRICE FOR
SIX DURING A COUNTY MATCH IN 1968

It is one of the better-known facts of my life in cricket that I was never coached. I learned from watching. The same is true of many other West Indian players of my time and before. Yet our batsmen have always been in the vanguard of the world's best players, improvisors playing an array of attacking strokes but with a correct defensive technique.

Playing from the front foot

For too many players today in all countries, the first line of defence is the pad. Too many players push the front foot down the wicket as the first line of defence. I always adhered to line and length without pushing out with the pad first. This is one of the fundamental flaws nurtured by modern-day coaches – particularly in England.

This type of coaching produces survivors and not real batsmen. These survivors tend to play exclusively from the front foot. Most of the great players have always been back-foot players, though there are those who say that Viv Richards was a front-foot player. When I first saw him he stayed very much on the back foot, playing back and across. In his last series in England he was still batting in this way. It is true that there was a period in the middle of his career when he became more of a front-foot batsman, but towards the end he went back to basics and started looking good again. Richards looked very comfortable at the end of his career and, of course, he has left a very impressive record.

West Indian batsmen have generally moved back and across their stumps a distance of 6–12 inches and waited to pick up the length of the ball. Today, a great number of them have gone front-footed – the work of coaches who have returned to the Caribbean after being taught overseas. In fact, I cannot think of any batsman, other than Brian Lara, who plays off the back foot like the majority of world-class batsmen. Frank Worrell, who perfected his technique in England, was slightly front-footed but also played back with equal facility. The likes of Clyde Walcott and Roy Marshall, a fine player who made his name as an opener for Hampshire and who continued to live in England until his death, played off the back foot. It gave them more time in which to see the ball and judge its length.

There are those coaches who teach players to get on the front foot before the ball is delivered. That, in my opinion, is the wrong approach. The choice of whether to move onto the front foot or to go back and across should be made when the ball leaves the bowler's hand. It is entirely up to the batsman to judge which way to play according to where the ball is pitched and not just stick the front foot down the wicket.

Most front-foot players, however, tend to extend themselves so far that they cannot move onto the back foot in time. The point about coaching is that it is easier for a coach to instruct cricketers to come onto the front foot: that helps them survive at the crease. Players find they stay longer at the wicket because it is more difficult for an umpire to give an lbw decision.

On the other hand, committing yourself to playing at a ball travelling at 90 mph off the front foot is asking for trouble. The batsman simply does not have enough time to readjust. Graeme Hick, when he came into Test cricket, was a case in point: he could get away with this in county cricket since there were not enough fast bowlers to bother him on account of his great height. He planted his front leg forward and played the ball around it. When the West Indies four-prong attack of fast bowlers came into being, caused effectively because there was no spinner good enough to replace Lance Gibbs, cricket was thrown into turmoil. Batsmen did not know how to handle it and were committing themselves too rashly.

Now that the likes of the Waughs and Alec Stewart and Mike Atherton – who came to the Caribbean as a front-foot player in 1994 and then altered his technique – have shown

31

they can handle this kind of bowling, it is a different matter. There are no express fast bowlers coming through in the Caribbean any longer and the upshot is that West Indian cricket, dominant for so long, will be affected that much more than other countries when defeats occur.

Tom Graveney, one of the master batsmen of my time, never committed himself on the front foot. He was never sticking his front foot a yard down the wicket: he always had room to play his shots. His method was based on where the ball pitched, unlike some of his colleagues, who were cramped and whose scoring area was restricted because of their premature commitment to the front foot.

Competition from other sports

The difficulty that cricket administrators and coaches now face in the West Indies is that, unless a youngster feels he has the chance of becoming a top cricketer – and how many do? – he will be drawn towards other sports and other channels. There is a great deal more money in other activities unless, of course, you are a Lara. It is also sadly the case that a lot of children do not bother to play any sport at all, even in such a lovely climate as the Caribbean. These boys and girls sit indoors with video games or computer games or simply watch television. For as long as I can remember, Barbados supplied the West Indies team with four or five players. Now they struggle to be represented at all.

All this has to do with the Americanization of the West Indies. In terms of monetary influence, West Indians have long veered towards the United States. I am a believer in a sportsman making as much money as he can while he can, for an athlete's life is a short and often hard one. Sports scholarships, particularly in basketball, naturally appeal to a young West Indian boy who is invariably from a humble family, even if this means going to live in the United States.

32

SIR GARY (TOP RIGHT) EXCELLED AT BASKETBALL IN HIS YOUTH,
BEFORE IT BECAME A PROMINENT SPORT IN BARBADOS

When I was growing up in Barbados, I could only have dreamed of the chance of playing basketball indoors. Other players who represented the West Indies when I did had just as much talent for football as they did for cricket, but there was no future in sports other than cricket. David Allan, who kept wicket in my time, was one of the first players to take up surfing standing up on a board. Had he been able to do this or wind-surfing for a living in the 1960s, he would probably have taken it up rather than played cricket. One of my own sons is keen on it now.

There are 14 sporting disciplines at the Sir Garfield Sobers Gymnasium in Wildey, St Michael, Barbados. These include swimming, tennis and an astroturf hockey pitch. There is a digital scoreboard, a separate players' entrance, excellent changing facilities and 5000 seats, which means it is used as a theatre and concert venue as much as a gymnasium.

Uniting the islands

I think it is possible that one day the West Indies will have its own football team, but not in my time. We might one day find a way of uniting all the islands, which would bring this about. The problem is that there are so many islands, mostly with small populations and a lack of finance. Trinidad, which in terms of cricket had nothing to shout about in the era between Sonny Ramadhin and Brian Lara, on its own has some very good football players – Dwight Yorke, who plays in the English Premier League with Aston Villa, is one. Indeed, they beat Aston Villa in 1994, but they are not Brazil. I would like to try to unite all the islands, but I can see that I would face some opposition.

The only reason the West Indies have always had a cricket team was that it came about before independence. This was despite the insularity that always existed and resulted, in the past, in some cricketers from the smaller islands not being

34

selected. The Windward and Leeward Islands always produced good players, but they were not always picked. This was
particularly unfortunate because some of them in the past
were better than those who are representing them today. In the
1950s and 1960s most of the players were chosen from the
islands that possessed Test grounds. A great deal of talent
resided in Barbados, who were good enough to stage a match
against a Rest of the World XI in 1967 and, indeed, good
enough to win it. But the occasion proved too much and we
were well beaten. This was a fixture criticized by Sir Frank
Worrell, who in his retirement stressed the need for regional
co-operation. I well remember his criticism that the fixture
would allow Bajans the opportunity to prove that they were
bigger than the West Indies. In the event, this did not happen.

CHAPTER 4

Advent of the One-Day Game

Cricket, like most other things in life, is subject to cyclic change. Interest in the game will flourish or wane depending on the magnetism of the dominant personalities at any particular time. The introduction of one-day cricket came at a time when crowds were at an all-time low and the county authorities had to find a way to rekindle public interest and keep their bank managers happy. One-day cricket was just the steroid that a faltering game needed at that time.

I was first approached to play county and one-day cricket by Ken Turner of Northamptonshire. Shortly after that, Ken Graveney from Gloucestershire approached me. I often wondered whether they knew something, since shortly afterwards, in 1968, the qualification requirement was changed. I was not prepared to accept the qualifying period that had hitherto been stipulated since it would have meant missing a couple of seasons with the West Indies.

The impact of overseas players

Those who approached me on behalf of their counties thought that one of the ways of bringing the crowds back was to sign some of the best overseas players who had great crowd appeal.

These were the days when counties were suffering financially and when, as the detractors used to say, the only person on the ground was a man with a white stick and a dog. This instant solution to the rapidly growing problem seemed to work, because, once the counties signed up the overseas players, the crowds started to return.

When I went to Nottinghamshire in 1968, I became one of the first overseas players to join an English county on special registration, that is, without going through the two-year qualification ritual before being eligible to play. According to the regulation, any overseas player wishing to join a county would have to be resident in the country throughout the year. That would have meant that I would have been unable to play for the West Indies during my qualifying years. I turned it down for the simple reason that no amount of money could have tempted me to abandon Test cricket, which has always been the most demanding level of the game.

It is a fact that I was always interested in county cricket but I would never have done anything that would threaten my place in the West Indies team or attract the anger and condemnation of the politicians and public. Of course, at that time we did not play so many Tests and one-day games and there was less chance of burning oneself out. Some players, out of economic necessity, went into League cricket in England, which was a lower level than the county game and which demanded no qualifying period.

It has always been my contention that, though often looked down on by the purists, League cricket improved my game because we played on some pitches which called for enhanced skills not just to succeed but often to survive. An inventory of the names of great West Indians who made a name for themselves in the Leagues and brought great glory to the game at Test level – such as Frank Worrell, Clyde Walcott and Sonny Ramadhin – proves the point. I started to play League cricket at the age of 21 for Radcliffe in the Central

Lancashire League. No one should underestimate the heavy responsibilities of an overseas professional, for he is not just the key player in the side but also the major attraction. It calls for great skill, a sound technique and considerable character, and it invariably raises the standard of one's game.

It was noticeable that in county cricket, the batsmen who came in from the Leagues were far more successful than the bowlers. Harry Pilling was a case in point. At the age of 13 he was playing as a leg spinner for Oldham in the Central Lancashire League. After joining Lancashire his batting developed to the extent that he was considered to be one of the best county batsmen never to have represented England, even though he was respected in county cricket. He was also one of the best leg spinners who never played for England. These days, more overseas players are in the Leagues but fewer English players seem to make the transition through the counties and into the Test teams.

I continue to encourage young players from the West Indies and other countries to try to play in England, in either the counties or the leagues. It is the best way of learning to play the moving ball in addition to acquiring the discipline of how best to play every ball on its merit. On hard, fast pitches outside of England, once the shine is off the ball it is not difficult to play shots, but in English conditions the ball can move, swing or seam throughout the day, demanding greater caution and skill.

Through standing firm and with the English public clamouring for the attractiveness of West Indians and other overseas players on the county circuit, the registration rule was changed in 1968. I was immediately offered contracts by Lancashire, Gloucestershire, Northamptonshire and Nottinghamshire. I signed for Nottinghamshire through my agent and longtime friend, Bagenal Harvey. I must admit that I was encouraged by the prospect of playing at Trent Bridge, the home of Nottinghamshire and one of my favourite grounds.

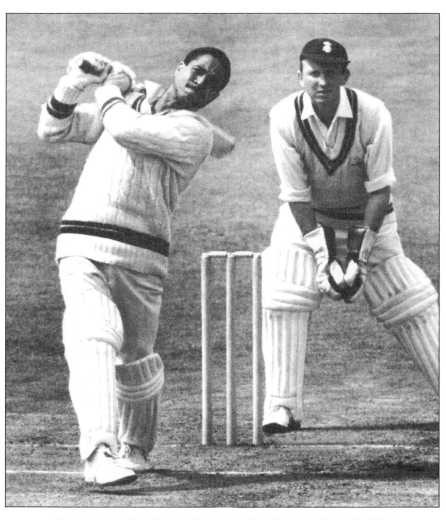

THE VALUE OF A FULL FOLLOW THROUGH. OPENING THE
SHOULDERS AGAINST PAT POCOCK AT THE OVAL IN 1968. ARNOLD
LONG IS THE WICKETKEEPER

It also appealed to me that they were then one of the weakest counties – perhaps *the* weakest one. I have always been one for the underdog. Playing for one of the strongest teams, say Yorkshire or Kent, would not have been so enticing, even if I might have had the odd day off!

Seven-days-a-week cricket

Having signed with Nottinghamshire, I was looking forward to having Sundays off to play golf and rest and recuperate from non-stop cricket from Saturday to Saturday. But that was not to be. With the introduction of the John Player League in 1969, top professionals in English cricket were expected to play a seven-day week, sometimes playing a straight 21 days without a break. Looking back on it now, I must have been temporarily insane to subject myself to that type of mental and physical torture. Fortunately, I survived without any noticeable short-term effects.

One of the reasons I had looked forward to golf on Sundays was because the fixture list was organized so badly that a considerable amount of time in the week was spent travelling between matches. As captain of Nottinghamshire, I was going to vote against the introduction of the Sunday League. But the players pulled me round to their way of thinking, saying that extra cricket would make for extra money. When this competition started, it was more of a hit-or-miss affair than it is today. Tailenders simply slogged to the boundary or were out. The likes of Colin Milburn and John Jameson struck the ball hard regardless of what form of the game they were involved in. I have never believed in saying that such and such a player is a one-day cricketer or a Test cricketer. A so-called "one-day specialist" should not be taking part in first-class competitions if that were the case. England have chosen to play Neil Fairbrother in the limited-overs game but not in Test cricket, in spite of the fact that he performed no worse than Graeme

40

Hick. With so many cricketers playing in one-day competitions day after day, why are some branded as specialists and some not?

I went into county cricket at the age of 31 and as captain of Nottinghamshire. Compared with what players get these days, my package of approximately £5000 a year salary, accommodation, a car and return air fares to Barbados seems paltry, even taking inflation into account. But I never grumbled and always gave it my best shot. It could never have been otherwise.

My presence in the team had the precise impact that the county authorities had hoped for – tremendous interest and enthusiasm. The crowds started coming back to follow Nottinghamshire. Every cricket crowd wanted to see the best cricketers in action, for at that time there was far less television coverage and hence the leading players were not so exposed to the limelight. Those were heady days but I sensed that certain players who wanted to be captain felt that their ambitions were dashed with my arrival on the county staff. Such are the vagaries of the game. I must say, however, that the hurt engendered by dashed ambitions never materialized into either overt or covert hostility.

About the same time that I started at Nottinghamshire, West Indies wicket-keeper Deryck Murray was on the playing staff. Other top West Indians in county teams around this time were Andy Roberts and Gordon Greenidge at Hampshire, Viv Richards at Somerset, John Shepherd at Kent, Keith Boyce at Essex and Rohan Kanhai and Lance Gibbs at Warwickshire.

The Cricket Cavaliers

The early pioneers of one-day cricket were the "Cricket Cavaliers", a group of overseas players in county cricket and professionals on county staffs. The Cavaliers team was the brainchild

NOT EVERY BALL WENT TO THE BOUNDARY, BUT THE INTENTION
WAS EVIDENT

of Bagenal Harvey who, in 1964, came up with the idea of putting together some of the most attractive performers in the game to play mainly 40-over matches, some of which were screened on BBC television and always drew huge viewing audiences.

Many good players who played for their national teams but were just short of Test standard, or who happened to play at a time when the pool of available Test players was of superior quality, were key men in the Cavaliers team. I can think of cricketers of the calibre of the Barbadian batsman Colin Blades and the Trinidadian Alvin Corneal. They were marvellous attacking batsmen who gave the crowds just what they came out to see. At most other periods in West Indian cricket they would have forced their way into the Test team.

We played mainly on Sundays and attracted crowds wherever we went. Many players looked forward to these games since some of the money generated helped to top up their benefits, which were substantially less than today. Cricket followers were also given an opportunity to see players in action who did not participate at Test, county or league levels.

Making the transition

As a West Indian, playing attacking cricket came naturally to me and, like the other West Indians who joined county sides, aggressive cricket was second nature. To me that was what the one-day game was all about. When I was growing up in the West Indies, I would go to the cinema in the morning on Saturdays and play cricket from 1.00 to 5.30 in the afternoon. Because there is no twilight in the Caribbean, we had no choice but to make quick runs since matches could not go on any longer. Yet there were many mature county players who found it difficult to make the transition from the three-day to the one-day game. I was fortunate enough to win the man of the match award in each of my first two one-day matches in

England in 1968, which got me off to a good start with Nottinghamshire. The Gillette Cup was the sole domestic one-day competition and thus was an enjoyable counterpoint to the county championship.

The following year, sponsorship by John Player helped to underwrite the success of the Sunday game and to establish one-day cricket as an attractive alternative to the dour diet of day-in, day-out county boredom. The Packer era was a natural development of the one-day game and, of course, one-day internationals are now institutionalized as a vital component of the itinerary of any foreign party as well as an important part of all fixtures.

Although there are so many different types of one-day cricket played now that a 40-overs competition is not going to make too much difference to a batsman's technique, I have always said that the one-day game should be the preserve of experienced players. Too often I have seen young players, with, I felt, tremendous potential, whose game was hindered rather than helped by playing limited-overs cricket.

In my view, because of the natural flair and attacking ability of West Indian batsmen, making the transition from three-day to one-day cricket was not as difficult or as traumatic as for English and some Australian players. That is why players like Alvin Kallicharran, Clive Lloyd, Viv Richards, Gordon Greenidge and Desmond Haynes were such successful drawing-cards. Haynes could still hit the ball in limited-overs cricket while concurrently struggling to excel in Test matches: it was a matter of the player adapting himself to changing circumstances.

Arrival of Kerry Packer

Having got the crowds back, English cricket still found it difficult to break away from its predominantly defensive tradition. At times I have seen captains and bowlers use the most

44

ridiculous field placing, ringing the boundary to curb free-scoring batsmen. The fact was that the laws permitted it. With the arrival of Kerry Packer on the cricketing scene, new rules made it mandatory to have fewer men in the circle, thereby restricting the defensive approach of the fielding side and making for more attractive cricket.

Packer gave one-day cricket a shot in the arm. I say this not because he employed me in a PR capacity but because I really do believe he was good for the game, as well as for the players. Cricket became a contest in which the bowlers and captains had to use their brains, rather than simply pushing all the fielders back to the boundary. I maintain that had I still been playing first-class cricket, I would have signed to play for Packer. Most of the time I would have been playing out of season and so still would have been able to take part in Test matches for the West Indies, assuming they still wanted me.

The other changes he brought about were exciting. I know that a lot of traditional people were upset about his introduction of coloured clothing. Yet not only did this become a fashion and make the game more attractive to females and non-cricketers, it identified the players properly. I came to accept it after a while and would not have objected if I had had to wear it. Anybody leaving the game at the ground or returning to their television set would immediately be able to identify which team was which. The Test and County Cricket Board and various individuals in England criticized coloured clothing – and eventually got around to taking it on board themselves. Coloured clothing is not likely to be adopted for Test matches but I am in two minds as to whether players' names on the backs of their shirts would be a good idea or not.

Inserting a camera in a stump was also Packer's initiative. He actually modified that part of the game and made it more enjoyable to watch as a result. Advising his fast bowlers to wear helmets was sensible, for top-class cricketers were involved in World Series and they played the game in a hard way. If they had not, they would have heard from him. I do not think he encouraged a gladiatorial contest – it was simply that there were no restrictions on short-pitched bowling, which, lest it be forgotten in England, began in the era of Larwood and Voce. Packer would call meetings if he saw that things were not going the way he wanted, although he had no need of my advice since he already had his advisers in place. My role was more to do with coaching and promotions in stores. And the trophy that was contested was named after me.

I found Packer to be a very pleasant, no-nonsense man. He was very keen on golf as well as polo at the time, played off a handicap of eight and asked me to help him with his swing. (I played off four in the 1970s, which, alas, has now gone up to nine.) I knew where I stood with him and he certainly let the players know that, contrary to its nickname, World Series was no circus. He made them realize what they were worth, and that they could be well paid for playing the sport they loved. Packer was a fair man. If they did their job well, he would look after them. I don't think my generation was unduly worried about poor pay at the time, for we were given the opportunity to travel and meet other people, but this was nothing by comparison with what the subsequent generation received from Packer.

Packer's initiatives

I do not go along with the theory that Packer hijacked international cricket – if countries wanted their players released, he would do so. The only country in which the game was affected was Australia, because so many of their top players were involved in his cricket that their Test team suffered. And he helped improve the lot of cricketers all the way down the line, from the star to the humble professional. I don't think anybody envisaged that the average player would ever earn any more than he was receiving in the 1970s, give or take a tiny increase owing to the cost of living. Yet that same player saw his earnings rise considerably more between the 1970s and 1990s than he did between the 1950s and 1970s. I don't think anyone would dispute now that this was all down to Kerry Packer.

As a direct result of Packer's involvement, Test match fees rose markedly and sponsors such as Cornhill were attracted to the game, backing England to the extent of pumping £1 million into the game over five years. Furthermore, the Test and County Cricket Board received £150,000 from Packer for the television rights for his Channel 9 coverage of the series between England and Australia in 1977. The smell of money was everywhere, and it all stemmed from Packer's disappointment that an offer he made to the Australian Board of Control for television rights had not been given the consideration he felt it merited.

From the point of view of the spectators, a contest between an Australian XI and a World XI would not have the same appeal as a match for the Ashes or the Wisden Trophy, unless, of course, the players involved could demonstrate that there was no difference in their commitment. This they showed to be the case. Pride was at stake and pride is a strong motivating force. The money was not exactly secondary because the individuals involved would not have been participating without it. But once on the pitch, each person was determined to show that he had been chosen on merit and that he could live in such company. Several players improved their game as a consequence.

In the High Court, it was declared that the attempts to ban from Test cricket any player contracted to World Series amounted to restraint of trade. The beneficial effects were seen – in addition to the financial rewards – as employment that was secure, regular and remunerative for more than 50 cricketers at a time when most of them would have no guarantee of even steady employment in the game. In Australia, talented players such as Ian Redpath and Ross Edwards returned

47

to the game. A coaching scheme for young players in New South Wales was initiated. And Mr Justice Slade declared that public interest had been heightened, in ways I have outlined. The downside was that court costs had to be borne which inevitably affected the finances of the game.

The reverse sweep

One of the good things about the one-day game, then as now, is that it makes batsmen devise new shots to penetrate defensive field placings off defensive bowling. The best known is the reverse sweep. I think the first batsman I ever saw attempt it was my old Pakistani friend Mushtaq Mohammad, who could also bat left-handed. Gordon Greenidge and Desmond Haynes played it quite successfully and often scored off it when to penetrate a heavily defensive field seemed impossible through orthodox strokeplay. In my day I tried quite a few new things but I never contemplated or attempted anything even remotely approaching the reverse sweep.

My philosophy always was that a bowler had to earn my wicket – I would not give it away. In my opinion trying to play the reverse sweep gives the bowler too much of a chance to hit the stumps or get the batsman out off a mistimed hit. When this comes off, it looks good. When, through playing it, the batsman is out, it looks terribly bad and often draws adverse comments about throwing away one's wicket. It is, in fact, the kind of shot that should be kept for exhibition games because you have to look at the "percentages" – the number of times it comes off. Some of the batsmen who try it can't even play conventionally, so I don't know how they can play behind themselves.

Even the textbook sweep shot is a guessing shot. Coaches who try to persuade batsmen to play the reverse sweep, as I understand Bob Woolmer has done, are looking for some kudos for themselves. The reason few West Indians try it is that

STILL ENJOYING THE GAME AFTER ALL THESE YEARS

they are sensible people. I have seen it played in a different way, a backhand shot with the intention of hitting a wide ball to square leg, but I would never try that either. I have tried to play the ball behind my back in benefit and exhibition games, but never when playing in earnest.

Technical adjustments

Since my retirement from the game in 1974, both batting and bowling standards have changed, and I would wager that a significant factor in this is the tremendous increase in one-day cricket. Limited-overs bowlers concentrate heavily on containment. Hence the preponderance of fast and medium-pace bowlers and the dearth of spinners. Even good or potentially good spinners are forced to compromise their natural tendency to give the ball air and have to settle for pushing it through flatter and quicker in their determination to restrict the scoring opportunities of the batsman.

Five-day Test cricket makes totally different demands on slow bowlers who, to get wickets, have to be able not just to impart spin, but must be able to flight the ball properly and vary their length, pace and amount of turn. That is the combination of skills which makes for a good spinner and makes a slow bowler such as Shane Warne a modern-day wonder to behold. The change of technique for fast bowlers is no less dramatic when moving from a strategy of containment in the one-day game to a more attacking strategy to get batsmen out in Test matches.

Yet though one-day cricket can be detrimental to cricketers, it remains a natural and necessary ally rather than an enemy of Test cricket and will continue to attract larger crowds wherever it is played. Though in recent years we have seen the emergence of a series of games in Sharjah dedicated to the one-day game, there should be no doubt in anyone's mind that Test match cricket is still the supreme form of the game, demanding the very highest levels of sustained skills and performance over a five-day period.

One-day cricket is here to stay. It brings much-needed revenue into the bank accounts of cricket administrations at both local and international levels and, most importantly, it has brought back the crowds and made everybody a winner. Having said that, however, I am not sure that the players themselves will benefit other than materially from the one-day game. When I watch the West Indian batsmen Phil Simmons and Philo Wallace at the crease, it strikes me that they are not used to building long innings. They play a disproportionate number of one-day games and need to take part in more three- and four-day games and make the necessary adjustments. I expect Simmons's game to get better now that he is playing county cricket. He remains, nonetheless, a very useful one-day cricketer.

On the whole, the one-day game does not help the development of class cricketers. Indeed, I have always contended that potentially good players can ruin their game by concentrating too heavily on one-day cricket. As I have mentioned, I do not believe youngsters have the experience to adapt their game and I cannot call to mind any batsmen who went into one-day cricket as dull performers and were transformed into being attractive to watch. The natural incubators for Test players are the three- and four-day games at county, state and regional levels where the emphasis is on playing oneself in and building an innings, rather than in the slapdash way that the one-day game seems to demand. This type of cricket is too much a game of chance for my personal liking.

Having said that, I also recognize the need to give the paying spectators one-day cricket since the gate receipts clearly indicate that this is what they will pay big bucks to see. So it is necessary to satisfy the demands of the public and, at the same time, protect the integrity of the players' technical skills. The way forward could be for countries to let their potentially good batsmen develop their techniques in the three- and four-day games before pitching them into one-day matches where they are forced to bat against the clock and take risks.

Another solution could be the selection of different teams to meet the demands of the one-day game and the longer matches. Of course, there will always be players good enough to play in both types of game while others will specialize in one or the other because they cannot meet the demands of patience, good concentration and sound technique on the one hand or cannot score as quickly as the situation demands and give their team the advantage of runs off a very limited number of overs. The problem with specialization is that most tours these days are a mix of one-day, four-day and five-day matches and few Boards of Control would wish to invest in a player whose contribution would be severely restricted, since moving players around is extremely expensive.

Night cricket

Limited-overs night cricket is another new development. This is something which has been experimented with in the Caribbean, notably in Trinidad, with pleasing results. I think we should have had night matches installed there a long time ago. In Barbados, a few games have been staged under flood-lights as money-making affairs – I myself have participated since I retired – only the lighting has not been that impressive. It has also been expensive. But it makes for a family affair and tourists enjoy it. I would only add that if West Indians go to watch this kind of cricket, they want to see competitive matches, not sky-larking.

The World Cup

It would be good to see a World Cup staged in the West Indies. England was the obvious initial choice and since then, of course, it has been held on the Indian sub-continent and Australia. South Africa is another ideal venue. Unquestionably, the first final in 1975 is still the one that stands out, partly because it was the first, but also on account of its being a thrilling match. Clive Lloyd and Rohan Kanhai, who held the West Indies innings together that day, played memorable innings. I could well have been in the team, but, alas, I was too badly injured to be anything other than a passenger.

The success of the World Cup is self-evident. In 1975, Ian Chappell, Australia's captain, regarded it as relatively insignificant, something to get out of the way before the more important cricket of the summer – a series against England, even though the Ashes were not at stake. By the time the fifth World Cup had finished in 1992, Imran Khan, the victorious captain, declared this to be the highlight of his career. The Pakistanis who toured Australia in 1995 likewise thought their Test series to be of less importance than winning the 1996 World Cup. Nevertheless, I still maintain that any Test series is the ultimate challenge and should be thought of as more significant than the World Cup.

No country has the right to call themselves world champions after winning a limited-overs competition; and the fact remains that limited-overs cricket is artificial cricket. It draws the crowds and television audiences and makes an immense amount of money. In other words, it is essential for the game. At one time, cricketers in Yorkshire, who liked to play in a hard and traditional manner, could not see the point of any one-day cricket. I have always seen it as a form of entertainment that does not in itself produce stars. It resurrected a dying game. But there is quite enough of it to be going on with.

CHAPTER 5

South Africa

Few things have pleased me more since I stopped playing than the re-entry of South Africa to world cricket. I am glad that, along with former cricketers Sir Colin Cowdrey and Richie Benaud and one of the most senior of cricket writers, Jim Swanton, I was able to make a contribution to bringing them back into the fold. South Africa had one of the best Test teams when they were forced out of world cricket in 1970. It would have been great for the game if the West Indies and South Africa could have played against each other before 1993.

There would have been two well-balanced sides with Graeme and Peter Pollock, Mike Procter, Eddie Barlow, Colin Bland and Dennis Lindsay appearing for South Africa against Wes Hall, Charlie Griffith, Lance Gibbs, Rohan Kanhai, Seymour Nurse, Conrad Hunte, myself and Jackie Hendriks, one of the best wicket-keepers I have ever seen. But because of its dehumanizing apartheid policies, the South African government incurred the wrath of the international community and deprived the world of seeing some very fine players. Both the South African public and the players lost a great deal because of the reprehensible behaviour of the ruling political elite.

Now that South Africa are back in the game, it is obvious that they will have a team to be reckoned with. In my view, if they had played more positive cricket they would have beaten the West Indies at Kensington Oval in 1993, just as they had managed to beat Australia in both Sydney and Johannesburg upon their return to international cricket. It is a major achievement to beat the fiercely competitive Aussies at home. Although they were beaten by England in 1994, the South Africans showed great strength, enthusiasm and determination and I would think that in four to five years they will have one of the top Test teams.

In the early stages of South Africa's re-entry to world cricket, do not expect any significant number of blacks and coloureds to make an impression. These groups took up soccer under the apartheid regime and I believe that it is more likely that blacks and coloureds will represent South Africa at the international level in soccer before cricket. I hope that when they do emerge in cricket, they will be good enough. Conrad Hunte, my old friend and colleague who now helps the development of the game in the townships, feels there is a great deal of latent talent. I think Omar Henry, the coloured left-arm spinner, did get into their team – the unofficial team that played Kim Hughes's breakaway Australians – on merit. But most of the coloureds have been so well attuned to soccer that they will find they are in a different world. They are inevitably going to need more tutoring than white boys who have grown up in the traditions of the game.

The sporting boycott

In trying to understand what was happening in South Africa when I was a player, one has to realize that the prevailing view among those who wanted to see change was that the best way to bring this about was to hit the South African government and the people of that country where it would really hurt. Sport is an important part of life in all countries. South Africa is blessed with a good climate and excellent sporting facilities, two prerequisites for the development and enjoyment of sport.

The South African people themselves are great lovers of a variety of sports and keep producing world-class sports personalities. When the world community therefore took the unprecedented step of excluding South Africa from world sport, it was a major blow, affecting them in an area where it was guaranteed to hurt most. Within South Africa itself there was a major outcry that the sports-crazy nation was robbed of the opportunity of being able to see their sporting heroes taking on the world because of policies which many whites were already criticizing as myopic and irrational. The sporting boycott of South Africa did as much to bring about fundamental change in the political life of the apartheid regime as the economic sanctions imposed by the United Nations.

I played with Ali Bacher as my partner in a double wicket competition in Rhodesia in 1970. I was ostracized by West Indian politicians and the public for that. We spoke often about South African players not being able to play Test cricket and the personal and collective hurt it caused. I had some idea of how they felt after the virulent brouhaha which followed my visit to Rhodesia. My pleas that I had put cricket above politics did nothing to stem the swelling tide of criticism which swept across the region. One Antiguan newspaper called me "a white, black man" and in Guyana both newspapers called for my sacking as West Indies captain.

The United Cricket Board

It is a great personal triumph for Ali, the former South African captain and now in charge of their United Cricket Board, to bring South Africa back into international cricket following the release of Nelson Mandela from prison, the collapse of the apartheid system and free and fair elections based on the system of one man, one vote.

For Mandela to come out of prison without feeling any vindictiveness, to become state president and behave as if nothing

56

DEMONSTRATING SOME OF THE FINER POINTS OF THE GAME IN
SOWETO

had happened to him shows what strength and discipline he possesses. When I met him on a visit to the Republic to celebrate the formation of the new United Cricket Board in 1991, he came downstairs in his bathrobe and spoke eloquently for 45 minutes, telling me what an honour it was for him to be with me, when in reality the honour was mine for being with him. He was well informed about the game and told me of his plans to visit the Caribbean.

It will always be difficult to separate politics from sport. Though in an ideal situation there should not be political interference, when government subventions fund many sporting bodies it may be unreasonable to deny that government the right to draw the line if it considers it necessary.

In the same spirit of reconciliation, Khaya Majola – in his youth a player who had been denied an opportunity to play the game, and who told Bacher at the height of Mike Gatting's 1989–90 breakaway tour that if he came to the townships in the Cape he would be greeted with a 15-inch tyre necklace – became the director of coaching of the new Board.

A day in Soweto

Although I was in the country for only a week during this 1991 visit, and it was difficult for me to concentrate with so many photographers around, I was impressed with the enthusiasm and also with the artificial facilities, which were kept nicely. One day, Sunil Gavaskar and I were taken to a field in Soweto that reminded him of the Bombay maidans, the park on which he had earned to play cricket. I bowled to him before a crowd of children and then brought a little calypso influence to bear on the children's singing.

I did see one teenage fast bowler that day in Soweto who put me in mind of Wes Hall; he was a 17-year-old called Walter Masemola who had been introduced to the game of cricket through the township development programme. I thought at

SHOWING YOUNGSTERS IN SOWETO HOW TO COVER
DRIVE IN 1991

the time that he might be a Test cricketer in the making, but when I last heard of Masemola, he was playing in 2nd XI cricket at the Wanderers. This is something that South Africans must come to expect, unfortunately: numerous young cricketers do not come on as expected.

Breakaway tours

In the 1980s one way in which certain people in South Africa thought they could give exposure to their own players who were starved of international competition – and at the same time satisfy the desire of their spectators to see world-class players – was by organizing a number of unofficial breakaway tours by teams comprising mainly West Indian, English, Australian and Sri Lankan players. They were universally criticized. In the West Indies and England in particular, the government, the public, the press, the churches and the cricket administrations all poured scorn on the players. The international community at the United Nations expressed its collective anger at what it saw as a deliberate attempt to circumvent the efforts to end apartheid in sport and to demolish the structures of apartheid in their entirety. Among the many very hard things said against the "rebel teams", the comment that sticks in my mind was that of Archbishop Desmond Tutu, who described Lawrence Rowe's team as "flannelled fools".

My approach to the issue was that one should not be judgemental and should seek to understand the precarious position of players whose futures were far from secure and who saw an opportunity to put themselves on a more financially viable footing. They found themselves in the same position that I had been in in 1970 – putting cricket first and politics second. They were paid much, much more than I received, however.

I myself had various offers to manage teams touring South Africa. Eddie Barlow, that fine all-rounder with whom I played for the Rest of the World, once asked me to visit South Africa as his guest. The fact that I refused had nothing to do with what was happening in the country. I had had my fill of publicity and criticism when I visited Rhodesia in 1970 and did not want to put up with all that again. Eddie and others knew that when my mind was made up, that was that. As a player, I had many invitations to play in South Africa, all of which I turned down.

Too few people seemed to realize at the time that the players themselves were convinced that playing in South Africa would be a great boon to the anti-apartheid lobby since white South Africans would get an opportunity to see accomplished blacks in action and would probably better understand that there was nothing innately inferior about them. In addition, not enough people understood that the conduct of the West Indian breakaway players, both on and off the field, was also likely to impress white South Africans and push them in the direction of change. This, all groups now agree, became a triumph of experience over hope. Those who initially were seen as villains were hailed eventually as pioneers of change and catalysts in the process of bringing black majority rule to a deeply divided country.

If I had felt that I could have helped the lot of the blacks and coloureds by going to South Africa myself, then I would have gone. I would have liked to have shown how the coloured person can behave. Surely if I could play in competition with white South Africans and do better than they did, then this was indicative to the politicians that players of all colours could and should compete on equal terms. Obviously I was anti-apartheid but I firmly believed first of all in an allegiance to my friends, not to political ideals. I reserved the right to tackle the problem of dismantling apartheid in my own way.

A great number of people in the Caribbean were behind the players who chose to go to South Africa, for they were not receiving much money at that time. Some of them felt they had been unfairly treated by the West Indies Board of Control. Others, such as Alvin Kallicharran, who was coming towards the end of his career, and Sylvester Clarke, who did not have an established place in the team, felt that this was a chance to make some money. They were from poor backgrounds and saw the chance of making the most of the talent they had been given. Lawrence Rowe, as the captain, received more criticism than any other player. In addition to being given a life ban along with the rest of the team, he was so ostracized in his native Jamaica that he had to go and live in Miami.

Playing Against South Africans

I first played against South Africans in 1963 in Australia when I took part in the Sheffield Shield competition for South Australia – and I must say that they were always very warm and welcoming to me. I suppose, however, it is difficult for someone like me to be a good barometer because I was accorded respect as an established Test cricketer. I also played for Rest of the World teams with a number of very good South Africans who had the potential to become outstanding Test players. In the 1970 team which played against England were Peter and Graeme Pollock, Barry Richards, Mike Procter and, of course, Barlow. We played as a multi-racial team – Indians, Pakistanis, West Indians and South Africans. Not only did we play together, we also shared the same dressing-room, something legally outlawed in South Africa.

Barry Richards once made a comment that will stick in my mind for ever. He said, "Gary, often I think that it would have been better if I had made less runs and made more friends." It was rough on the players that they had to pay such a heavy price for the policies of their errant government. Frankly, I do not think that anyone could have envisaged that they would have remained in the cricket wilderness for such a long time.

A WEST INDIAN BOWLING THE CHINAMAN TO A SOUTH AFRICAN.
AN EAGER CROWD GATHERS IN SOWETO

Whenever I spoke with South Africans, there was always a certain melancholic ring of regret in their voices that they and the people of South Africa had sacrificed so very much on the altar of assumed racial hegemony.

New opportunities for West Indians

One of the most moving experiences of my life was when I arrived at Johannesburg Airport in 1991 and was warmly and tearfully embraced by Graeme Pollock. There were feelings of mutual pleasure at the renewal of an old friendship. Deep in our hearts there was much more that words could never express. I often think that West Indian followers of the game are the poorer for not having seen the great South African players of my era in action. So, too, the South African spectators were robbed of seeing my West Indian contemporaries. Thankfully, the face of South African cricket is changing as the country itself is changing. With the dismantling of apartheid and the re-entry of South Africa to world cricket, many West Indian players are now playing club cricket there with outstanding success. Fortunately, the exodus of our players is likely to have less impact on West Indian cricket than the exodus during the English season, since the South African summer coincides with the close season in the Caribbean.

With the English counties cutting back on overseas players, more West Indians are likely to go after playing opportunities in South Africa. Because of very good financial inducements and superior facilities, as well as the potential for coaching a new generation of enthusiastic youngsters, I predict that a better class of player will be going there in the future, not only to earn a good living but also to help raise the level of interest in the game in the black townships. Whereas the English authorities feel that the presence of overseas players on county staffs was detrimental to their cricket, the South Africans are rushing to embrace them in the belief that both the game and the individual players will benefit from rubbing shoulders on and off the field. The value of including overseas players in their domestic cricket is already apparent.

Some people were surprised that when South Africa came back on the international scene in 1992, the standard of their cricket was still relatively high. I was not surprised. After all, for years their skills were being honed and tested against the so-called "rebels" – Lawrence Rowe, Alvin Kallicharran, Collis King, Franklyn Stephenson, Sylvester Clarke, Ezra Moseley and others of Test calibre. In 1993, when the South African team made its first historic tour of the West Indies, Conrad Hunte brought a youth team to play in Barbados. I had the pleasure of lecturing to them at Kensington Oval on the morning before the Test match started and was very touched by both their knowledge and interest. The tour was an outstanding success and laid the foundation for follow-up tours in the future. Perhaps there could even have been one or two future Test players in Conrad's youth team.

One of the great joys about my visit to Soweto was to see hundreds of youngsters – black, coloured and white – playing cricket together. Quite the most amazing thing, however, was that all of the coaches were women. It was explained to me that among the black population soccer rather than cricket was the preferred sport and most of the male coaches gravitated to coaching soccer, thereby leaving the way open for female coaches to look after cricket. After listening to them and watching them in action, I must say that they certainly seemed to know what they were doing.

CHAPTER 6

The Drag and the Bat

Growing up in a cricket-crazy environment in the West Indies, my brothers and I, together with a number of boys from my district, played the game from sun-up to sun-down. We also played a variety of other games – football, basketball and table tennis as well as indoor games – but cricket was king. Our role models were invariably drawn from the field of sport and every boy wanted to be a Weekes, Walcott or Worrell, a Learie Constantine or George Headley. In those days the game was known to one and all as "bat and ball". Today, when I think of cricket and the multitude of changes the game has undergone, I return to the fundamental fact that it remains predominantly a game of bat and ball. The key players are still the batsman and the bowler, and the equipment is still the bat and the ball.

The front foot rule

Nor are the rules that govern the game today significantly different from when the game first started almost three centuries ago. One rule that has changed for the better is the front foot rule. This was introduced to curb what was known in the game as a "dragger" – a bowler who gained himself an unfair advantage by dragging his foot through the crease. What this did was, in reality, to shorten the pitch, since instead of delivering from 22 yards, with the drag they would deliver from about 20 yards.

Two of the more obvious draggers during my playing days were the Australian Gordon Rorke and the great English fast bowler, Freddie Trueman. They tormented English batsmen in Test and county cricket respectively – batsmen who, with a few notable exceptions like Ted Dexter in later years and Derek Randall, were not good at handling pace. I remember my good friend Colin Cowdrey complaining one day that if he played forward, Rorke's front foot would land on his.

The draggers also made life very difficult for the umpires, who had that split second less time to make a decision about both the bowler sending down a no-ball and a batsman surviving an lbw shout.

So the bowlers took advantage of the situation. Thankfully, West Indian bowlers were not draggers. Our boys planted their feet in the right place. I often thought when I watched some of the draggers that if they were part of a West Indian team under my captaincy, they would have to sort out their technique or be dropped from the team. That was my abiding credo, and I think my players were inspired by my example. The new front foot rule is good for fair play and good for the batsmen and umpires. Discerning observers of the game would have noticed that some "quicks" lost a few yards of pace when the new rule was enforced.

The Australians felt that keeping the back foot behind the bowling crease should remain the factor determining a no-ball. The feeling in England was that the front foot should land behind the popping crease and that the Australian solution permitted a legalized drag, which would give the bowler with a long stride an unfair advantage. There was also the possibility of the pitch becoming damaged at the point where the bowlers grounded their feet just behind the popping crease. The front-foot experiments continued, until in 1962 the

Imperial Cricket Conference, as it was then called, agreed unanimously that all countries would utilize this front-foot method in all first-class cricket.

A bowler such as Freddie Trueman was fortunate that this rule did not come about until his career was nearly over, for he wanted to put his front foot, he said, "where it would really count". Neither Wes Hall nor Charlie Griffith, when they came to England with the 1963 West Indies party, wanted to play under this new legislation. And Freddie said that many batsmen thought bowlers would be in short supply because of the number of tests they had to pass before they could qualify!

Limitations on bowlers

Such limitations on bowlers, including restricting the captain in the field to having just two men behind square on the leg side, have meant that it is hard to make a comparison of records today with those created in the past. Obviously it was more difficult to score runs if a bowler such as Harold Larwood concentrated on "leg theory" with a string of short legs and leg slips, or if Trevor Bailey looked to contain batsmen by concentrating his attack in that area with a packed on-side field. When I faced Keith Miller and Ray Lindwall in the '50s, they bowled to what they called a "carmody field" – named after a former Australian captain, Keith Carmody – which was similar to the "umbrella" placings of gully, three slips and three leg slips. Cliff Gladwin bowled off-cutters on green pitches at Derby with four or five fielders behind square. Today, he would have to start his off-cutter from wide outside off-stump because he would not be protected by sufficient fielders on the leg side.

Frankly, I sometimes think that the game – with the exception of the front foot rule – should have been left the way it was. When I am in the commentary box, I frequently wonder where the rule-makers are going with the rules. Often I have sat in the stands at Lord's, Sydney or Kensington Oval and reflected that the only thing in this world which is permanent is change, and wondered which rule or piece of equipment they would change next.

I admire bowlers. I wonder how many people realize that all of the new rules introduced in the last 30 years favour batsmen. The limit placed on the number of short-pitched balls a bowler can send down per over, the limitation on field placings, the introduction of protective gear for batsmen – helmets, arm pads, thigh pads and chest pads – are all for the batsman's benefit. The only rule change which favours the bowler is the lbw rule. All of the other changes have tilted the game in favour of the batsmen.

Heavy bats

The many changes the game has undergone have also affected bats. Today's bats are heavier than in my playing days. When I played, bats weighed 2 lb 4 oz to 2 lb 5 oz. Now they weigh up to 3 lb. They are also now remarkably thick. This, it is claimed, makes it more difficult for the bowler to hit the fine edge, which, literally, is a thing of the past. The likes of Ian Botham and Graham Gooch strike the ball so hard with these great railway sleepers that, when a bowler does find the edge, the ball is likely to fly anywhere at great speed. I have seen Botham topedge an intended hook and the ball has still gone for six. These batsmen have made the game less artistic and batting less felicitous. Wristiness has gone out of the game, except on the subcontinent. Such batsmen prefer to try to smash the ball through cover rather than dexterously late cut it to third man. Heavier bats are also the reason why the hook shot is not played so well or so freely as it was in the past. Denis Compton used to say that he liked his bat to feel as if it were a wand. Inevitably, then, plenty of coaches who played the game in his era deplore the fact that some players, especially young boys, are wielding bats that are too cumbersome for them. This is partly a legacy of the one-day game.

When I am asked whether I would have used the various pieces of equipment now available had they existed in my day, the answer is always no. I put my trust in the natural gifts God gave me and the skills I acquired through time. If, as a batsman, I could not take on the best the world had to offer and feel confident against them, I would have dropped out of top-class cricket and played at a different level.

Extra protection

Today, most players, in spite of wearing helmets, still get hit. In fact, more batsmen have been hit when wearing helmets than when not wearing them. Batsmen seem to think that because of the helmet they don't need to take evasive action against the short-pitched ball. I cannot envisage myself – even in the days when the eyes were not as alert, the reflexes not as sharp and the feet not as quick as they once were – going out to bat in a helmet and with all sorts of artificial aids padding up my body. Such things are not for me. Sometimes cricketers give the impression that they are going out to do battle or are off to Mars. They are weighed down by all this protection and have a lack of confidence in themselves. This embraces a lack of judgement or a concern that they will be hit. A batsman is supposed to be able to get out of the line: he has pads to keep the ball away from his legs and even they should be used only as a second line of defence. It used to irritate me when a good batsman like Colin Cowdrey became obsessed with pushing out at the ball with his pads and not making full use of his ability. And even this extra protection is no guarantee against injury: I remember on a visit to India seeing Manoj Prabhakar hit on the visor and still having his nose broken.

That is why I have always set Ian Chappell, Clive Lloyd, Viv Richards, Richie Richardson and Larry Gomes apart from all the other batsmen in the last decade. They took on the best fast bowlers in the world without any extra protective gear and were highly successful. Ian, who deserved to be ranked as a great batsman, did wear a helmet on occasion at the end of his career and I noticed that Richie had one on throughout West Indies' 1995 tour to England. I can sympathize with the need for this when a batsman's reflexes are not what they were. But this does not alter my view that if Ken Barrington had sheltered behind a helmet when the West Indies had played against him, we would never have got him out.

I understand, however, why the modern batsman feels he must wear all of the protective gear available on the market. Players today, many of whom, in all honesty, fall short of the skills of those of my generation, earn big money from the game. Imran Khan told me once that decent cricketers do not want to be put out of the game through injuries resulting from not wearing protective gear, since they would lose money. I can sympathize with the top player who understandably wants to remain fit. Temporary injury means a temporary loss of earning capacity. Permanent injury could result in the perma-nent loss of a substantial livelihood and a secure financial future for the player and his family; there are not many oppor-tunities available even for the very gifted players after they have retired from the game. The West Indian attack obviously causes batsmen to wear helmets, although in the mid-1990s I do not see any terrifying fast bowlers around.

Helmets

The helmet came into the game after the advent of World Series Cricket, although it was patented by a batsman, Mike Brearley, who was not involved in the World Series. The Eng-land captain came up with the idea of wearing a skull cap against Australia in 1977 and then wore a crash helmet against the much weaker Indians and Pakistanis, who possessed nobody quicker than medium pace. I do, of course, recall when Nari Contractor, the captain of India, fractured his skull in Barbados in 1962 and had to undergo brain surgery that saved his life. However, considering the number of very fast balls bowled in Test cricket, the occasions when batsmen were hit were few and far between. If anything, the advent of the helmet has meant that the number of bouncers bowled at all batsmen, even tailenders, has increased. A fast bowler will be less concerned about inflicting injury if he sees that a number 11 batsman is trussed up like the Michelin Man.

Those facts of life temper my views. Today's players wish to ensure that nothing stands in the way of maintaining their places at the top for as long as is humanly possible. The protective gear acts like an insurance policy against disability and loss of earnings. Batsmen always tell me that the extra protection makes them feel more confident and secure. But all I ever needed to protect myself was the basic equipment – bat, pads and gloves. I did not even wear a thigh pad, having found it uncomfortable early in my career. I cannot recall ever being hit badly on my thigh. The basic equipment served me well and provided adequate protection.

I never sustained any serious injury while playing through being struck with a ball, although I well recall being hit in the face once. It was by a short ball from Richard Jefferson, a Cambridge University medium-pacer, in a match at Lord's in 1961. I had two teeth knocked out and needed to have 11 stitches in my mouth. The ball came out of the murky pavilion and the photograph of the incident made me look as if I had been decapitated, but there was no serious injury. So long as the batsman is able to pick up the length and direction of the ball as soon as it leaves the bowler's hand, he should be able to hook or sway out of the line.

There was only ever one occasion when I was at all concerned about being hit. That was when I had to face Dennis Lillee, who was bowling as quickly as I ever saw him bowl, on a rock-hard pitch at Perth in 1971–72. The surface became damp overnight and Dennis started to bounce the ball over the batsman's head off a length. I went to the crease with the Rest of the World XI having mustered 46 for 5, was beaten by the first ball I faced without having time to play a shot, and gloved the next one to Rodney Marsh. Normally I hated to be out, but not on this occasion.

Arm guards, pads and gloves

Arm guards provide still further protection, but I'd have thought they would have been of greater necessity on green pitches in the 1950s than they are now. On some days then it was not possible to distinguish the pitch from the square. Since arm guards did not exist, you quickly learned how to play in those conditions. You had to play the ball on its merits – you knew that if you made runs consistently, you were a good player. I don't think I would enjoy batting in England now as much as I did then. Only a good batsman made runs in those circumstances. It's a shame now that such a pitch is reported as soon as the ball starts to move around, for cricketers used to look forward to playing in those conditions.

Two changes that are decidedly for the better are the introduction of a light pad that can absorb the impact of being hit by the ball, and the improved design of pad straps. At times in the past batsmen were given out caught at the wicket when in fact the ball had come off the buckle; although this never happened to me, I knew players who were given out for this reason. Sometimes batsmen – including myself – had to change their pads because the buckles were loose. I always selected the pads I wore with lightness and comfort in mind. Rather than being concerned about straps hanging loose, I would cut off the ends.

As for batting gloves, these are now more securely designed than of old, but the problem of broken fingers remains. The experiment with the kind of one-piece glove that Tony Greig wore came and went. Foam makes for considerably better padding than rubber, although that lasted in the form of spiked gloves for years. In recent seasons, injuries have arisen through fingers becoming trapped against the bat handle. Special finger guards have been designed and manufactured to try to prevent this, but it can reduce the flexibility of the grip.

When England set out for South Africa in 1995, Alec Stewart took with him five pairs of a special hexalite protector, worn over the glove, to prevent his fingers from jamming against the bat handle. Gray-Nicolls were so taken with this that they decided to include it in their catalogue and suggested to Brian Lara that he try it out in the nets. But Brian was not so impressed. He is such a good batsman that he hardly ever gets hit on the glove!

Surviving – then and now

I sometimes like to speculate on how some of the modern wonder boys would have taken on the likes of Frank Tyson (probably the fastest bowler I have seen), Roy Gilchrist (the most dangerous), Wes Hall, Charlie Griffith, and Freddie Trueman. I believe that in my playing days the pitches were quicker, which was not for the comfort of those afraid of pace. It is obvious that some of today's players must think we were crazy facing terrifying quicks on faster pitches without helmets, chest pads, thigh pads and arm pads. Sir Frank Worrell used to go out to bat against Trueman and Brian Statham with a towel stuffed down his trouser leg to protect his thigh. Brian Close would rather have been hit on the chest by Wes or Charlie than fence at the ball and possibly edge it to the wicketkeeper or slip cordon. Even by the mid-1970s Colin Cowdrey's only form of protection was still foam rubber. He wore this underneath his shirt against us in the Caribbean in 1959–60 and later against Dennis Lillee and Jeff Thomson on fast, bouncy pitches in Australia after he had been called out to join MCC's tour at the age of 42. Colin McDonald, the Australian opener, was not as gifted as the others I have mentioned, but he took all that was flung at him without complaint, opting for a waistcoat protector only towards the end of his career. To survive called for sheer courage and good technique – fundamental characteristics which were far more plentiful at the time when I played.

CHAPTER 7

Technique

The 1960–61 series between West Indies and Australia was the best I ever played in. Frank Worrell and Richie Benaud were exceptional captains and both teams played outstanding cricket, impressing both on and off the field. Sir Donald Bradman was immensely appreciative and was instrumental in getting me a contract to play for South Australia in the Sheffield Shield.

Sir Donald was impressed by my technique and approach to the game and thought that having me play for South Australia would be a good opportunity for the young players in Australia to see a Test cricketer from another country in action. I hope the youngsters benefitted from my presence in the team. My game was certainly helped by my time with them. It used to amuse me to hear people – especially the so-called experts and cricket purists – say that I had a "flawed technique". I would like to think that my best answer to those buffers was my innings of 254 at the Melbourne cricket ground in the 1971–72 series between Australia and Rest of the World, which was described by Sir Donald as probably the best innings ever played in Australia. Isn't there a biting irony in the fact that young players were being coached to emulate a batsman with a "flawed technique"? Or was it that they were being shown how *not* to bat?

SHARING A DRINK WITH SIR DONALD BRADMAN IN
MELBOURNE

As already mentioned, I was never coached. I had a simple approach, based on the theory that if a batsman picked up the ball early enough he could position himself to play whatever shot he thought the ball deserved. Sir Donald always advised players to watch the position of the batsman's body and his feet. After seeing the coaching film made of my innings of 254, Seymour Nurse, the West Indian stylist who was my playing contemporary for many years, once said to me, "But Gary, I didn't know you were so correct." The point, as Seymour recognized, is that technique is only critical in defence. To become a good batsman, your defensive technique must be correct.

Herman Griffith, the West Indian fast bowler who had the distinction of bowling Sir Donald for a duck, once made the observation that, "We all walk, but some of us walk differently." The ability to improvise is what sets the great batsmen apart from the merely good ones. Viv Richards, who had a quick eye and picked up the ball very early, was a master of improvisation. He was better than most at latching onto the ball outside the off stump and putting it through the arc between mid-on and backward square leg. There were few more exciting batsmen than Viv on the attack.

But when Viv was on the defensive it was obvious to the discerning eye that he had a problem with his technique. I noticed early on that in defence his bat was never perpendicular but rather semi-perpendicular. His bat handle tended to point towards mid-on or mid-wicket, always giving the bowler an extra chance to penetrate his defence. Later in his career his defence improved tremendously and he played with a much straighter bat, pointing the handle towards the line of the ball instead of towards mid-wicket as I had observed during the World Series Cricket in Australia.

Of the batsmen I played with, Conrad Hunte, the West Indian opener, was the most technically correct. Rohan Kanhai had a good technique in defence while he gave the world the improvised falling sweep shot. I didn't see it before and I have not seen it since. That was Rohan's unique gift to the game. Other players whose techniques were sound were Everton Weekes, Frank Worrell and Clyde Walcott of the West Indies. So, too, were those of England's Colin Cowdrey, Peter May, Tom Graveney and Ted Dexter. Although Colin's technique was impressive, he too often used more pad than bat. Ted, on the other hand, delighted in putting bat to ball. He played like a West Indian and was one of the best English batsmen I ever saw.

The Australian opener Bobby Simpson also had a good technique, as did his countrymen Ian and Greg Chappell, and the South Africans Graeme Pollock and Barry Richards. Simpson and Pollock each had a major weakness – they did not cope well with the short-pitched ball.

The real master

For me, one of the greatest of all batsmen with an outstandingly impressive technique was the Indian maestro, Sunil Gavaskar. He played against the world's best bowlers, fast, medium and slow, and scored more runs than any other batsman of his time. His technique was superb and he was the batsman one never relished bowling against. A Trinidadian calypsonian, Lord Relator, immortalized Gavaskar's technical astuteness and overall genius when he sang, "Gavaskar, the real master, bat broad like a wall, they couldn't out Gavaskar at all." How true. The record shows he scored 10,122 runs including 34 Test centuries.

Significantly, he scored most of his runs outside of his native India with its notorious slow wickets. One measure of his greatness is the fact that he made consistently high scores over ten years playing in all countries except South Africa. Sunil was no flash in the pan. He was not limited in his range of shots, either. He played every one and was always in full control. Like all of the great players, he dictated to the bowler what he should bowl and not the other way around.

Another player whose technique I greatly admired was the Jamaican batsman Lawrence Rowe. He was immensely talented and could have become one of the very great batsmen. His potential was obvious when he scored a century in his first Test and a double century in his second. His 302 at Kensington Oval was one of the best knocks I have ever seen and won him the popular acclaim of the Barbadian crowd, one of the most critical in the world.

Favourable impressions

Who has particularly impressed me over the last 20 years? Apart from Ian Chappell – for whom I have an even higher regard than for his brother Greg – I had a considerable respect for Doug Walters, who always looked to attack the opposition's bowling and was a particularly formidable batsman on the hard pitches in Australia. Mark Taylor, Michael Slater and Mark Waugh all did well in the Caribbean and I think David Boon, who had a lot of guts and a good technique, was very much underrated.

Of English batsmen, Alec Stewart is a no-nonsense, class player and Mike Atherton has proved he has a sound technique, endurance and a good brain. Graeme Hick has at last begun to make runs but still has a long way to go.

India have produced two class players in Kapil Dev and Sachin Tendulkar but I feel Mohammad Azharrudin is susceptible to the quicks. Javed Miandad was vital to Pakistan because he was capable of playing the long innings and has a tremendous record, averaging more than 50 in Test cricket. I was impressed with one of his successors, Basit Ali, when he came to the Caribbean.

Despite the Pakistan team's problems, they still possess some match-winning bowlers. Wasim Akram and Waqar Younis are two very useful performers, although the fact that they can achieve reverse swing with an old ball is nothing new.

MEETING ALEC STEWART, A BATSMAN SIR GARY ADMIRES, AND
MATTHEW MAYNARD (RIGHT) AT KENSINGTON OVAL,
BARBADOS, IN 1994

WHICH WAY IS IT GOING TO TURN? SIR GARY IN ONE OF HIS
SLOWER STYLES IN ENGLAND IN 1969

It is a matter of disciplining yourself, because a good batsman watches the bowler's hand when he comes up to the wicket. Years ago in Guyana there was a medium-fast bowler called Ramnarez who could achieve reverse swing without knowing he was doing so or being able to control the ball. He never played for the West Indies.

I remember that in England on the West Indies' 1963 tour Freddie Trueman bowled me with what he intended to be an away swinger, only for it to come back into me. He told me afterwards that he did not know what had happened. For me, reverse swing worked on occasion. I always tried to counter the batsman with something different – it was that kind of approach which made a bowler a cut above the rest. Sometimes the ball would go in a different direction from what I had intended, but most of the time I knew what I was doing. If ball-tampering does exist to the extent that has been suggested, then that can certainly assist reverse swing.

The Pakistanis also possess a decent leg-spinner in Mushtaq Ahmed, although clearly Shane Warne is the better bowler. Warne is a big spinner of the ball, although no more so than Dave Sincock, who played with me for South Australia. Sincock had one of the best disguised googlies but could never pitch it very accurately. My grouse with Shane is that he always bowls round the wicket into the rough. Gupte, Benaud, Intikhab and Abdul Qadir, for a while, all bowled over the wicket. Shane will not worry a top-class batsman who thinks about the game. He relies too much on a batsman making mistakes, and tries to bowl batsmen round their legs. But I like his attitude and his determination.

CHAPTER 8

Developments On and Off the Field

As well as alterations to the laws of cricket, there have been many other changes to the game since I retired, some more worthwhile than others.

Umpiring standards

Umpiring standards are generally higher than they were 25 years ago, and the job is better paid today and offers more incentives in the way of trips abroad. If I were asked to nominate the finest umpires of my own time, I would mention Col Eagar, Charlie Elliot and Syd Buller. Today, Dickie Bird, Venkat and David Shepherd, all of whom I played with, are most probably the best. They are respected partly because they played a great deal of cricket.

I don't think the gap in pay between umpires and players will be narrowed completely. The public come to see players, not umpires, who are not in physical danger unless the ball is hit hard straight back at them. As for the umpiring in Pakistan, everybody who goes there returns to their own country and complains about the decisions given against the visiting team. But it is not always the touring side which suffers, nor is it the case that the English umpire's verdict should be accepted ahead of the Pakistani umpire's. When I played on the Indian sub-continent, I found that decisions were made genuinely – even the bad ones. The umpires had just not had as much experience of top-level matches as the English umpires had.

It is not a job I would ever have enjoyed. Teams go out to the middle with the notion of putting pressure on the umpires. At team meetings beforehand they all decide to go up for a decision: I am sure this is genuinely planned in advance. The team playing on its home ground so often seems to get the decision in its favour. The umpire in question has to depend on his courage, strength of purpose and knowledge.

Umpires also have to deal with batsmen who choose not to "walk" if they have edged a catch, although I do not regard this as cheating. I see it as a matter of conscience: I did not want to remain at the wicket knowing I was out. Above all, a batsman must be consistent, which is to say he either walks or he does not. Those who do not can fairly say that the umpire is there to make a decision, so long as they do not try to hoodwink him by building up a reputation for walking and then being selective about doing so. There were only a few walkers when I played and now there are very few indeed because there are more incentives in the game.

The third umpire

One significant innovation for the improvement of the game which can erase ill-feeling over umpiring decisions is the introduction of the "third umpire". Using a television monitor, he can now adjudicate with precision on run-outs, stumpings and hit wicket appeals when called upon by the umpire in the middle. I believe that having a third umpire is a good move – up to a point. Run-outs and stumpings can clearly be judged from television replays. That can only enhance the umpire's judgements. But a third umpire should not become involved in making decisions over lbw appeals. Those can most properly be judged in the middle. If too many decisions are made from beyond the boundary, the flow of the game will continually be interrupted. The role of third umpire should be for people who are constantly engaged in umpiring. At every ground there is a reserve official who is called upon if either of the two umpires is injured, so he should be given the task.

I would strongly urge that proper consideration be given to the use of the camera to assist the umpire in making a decision on catches that are doubtful. Once in 1995 when I was working for Voice of Barbados, covering the Test at Bridgetown between West Indies and Australia, all of us in the commentary box believed that Steve Waugh had caught Brian Lara, until the TV cameras showed otherwise. I don't believe Steve realized what had happened. If there had been no television cameras present, then everybody would have been happy; as it was, the slow motion replay put doubt into viewers' minds as to the legitimacy of the catch and the conduct of the fielder. If the camera is in place, why not use it for these decisions? It is not going to tell lies – except in the movies. The third umpire could then put all our minds at ease and there would be no sense of aggravation between the teams.

The drawback to all this, of course, is that the umpire standing in the middle can have his authority eroded. Once an official lacks confidence, it is not easily restored.

Ball boys

I noticed during England's tour of the West Indies in 1994 that young boys were employed on the boundary to retrieve the ball and throw it back to the nearest fielder. This is one of the changes to the modern game of which I strongly disapprove. It was a natural aspect of cricket when I played that the batsman would hit the ball to the boundary, and the fielder would run after it, pick it up and throw it back. This, of course, was guaranteed to add to the fatigue of the fielding side. It is a natural part of the game and contributes to keeping a competitive edge and making players try harder to keep fit. John Arlott, the great commentator, used to wax lyrical about how Frank Worrell would first lean on his shot, then bisect the field and make the fielders chase after the ball – which was always going to beat them to the boundary. It was all part of Frank's magic. Not only did it look good, it also sapped the fielders' energy.

I suggest that the International Cricket Council should take a look at the deployment of these boys. There is an argument that having retrievers on the boundary helps to speed up the game. That may be so, but in my view it is a retrograde step which gives the fielding side an added advantage that cannot be justified. Fielders should at all times have to retrieve the ball from the boundary. West Indian players generally hit so many boundaries that the use of ball boys would give their opponents an unfair advantage. On the other hand, those teams who score their runs with fewer boundaries, compiling their runs in singles, ones and twos, would tend to tire out their opponents, even though their scores may be smaller.

What I saw creeping into matches could spread throughout the cricketing world if an early stop is not put to it. Indeed, the only individuals who should have access to the field of play and the ball should be the 13 players and two umpires. I see the use of ball boys as a form of crowd interference, which has become a very sensitive issue these days. The incident in Guyana during the 1994 West Indies/England one-day match – which the West Indies claimed they had won but which was called a draw by Raman Subba Row, the match referee, because of crowd interference – is still sufficiently fresh in the mind to advise caution about any extraneous persons encroaching on the field of play.

Fitness

All cricketers and the authorities must be concerned about the plethora of injuries which continue to cripple players today, particularly fast bowlers. Curtly Ambrose had to miss the 1994 West Indies tour of India because of recurring problems from an overworked shoulder while his team-mate, Ian Bishop, remains out of Test cricket because of back problems. Like Bishop, Waqar Younis's future is in doubt because of a stress fracture of the back. His team-mate, Wasim Akram, has had surgery on his knees. Darren Gough had to leave Australia prematurely while on the crest of a wave during the 1994 tour – this was because of a foot injury – and Craig McDermott's torn ligaments in his left ankle put him out of the 1995 Australian tour of the West Indies before the first Test match.

The normal demands of cricket have always put a high premium on optimal fitness as a prerequisite for good performances on the field. The addition of a physiotherapist to the permanent staff of most Test teams has helped modern-day players to maintain their physical fitness through organized programmes of strict fitness regimes.

Frankly, some of the exercises I see players having to undergo seem quite unnecessary. Too much emphasis is placed on running and not enough on stretching and squatting, which are exercises that tone up the muscles and are more conducive to playing better cricket. There has been a tendency for coaches to ape football managers. I noticed that when Micky Stewart and Graham Gooch were in charge of England, too much time was spent on physical exertion – possibly as a result of their interest in football. This approach does not suit every player: imagine asking Peter May and Colin Cowdrey to lap a ground before the start of play, or even after it! They would not have become better batsmen as a result. Similarly, David Gower's game was not improved by these methods. Good batsmen whose game encompasses a sound technique and a sense of timing will not be helped by being asked to perform like some strapping centre-forward in the English Premier League. It was no wonder that Gower grew to resent being treated like an automaton and retired from the

The Sobers cover drive, described by CLR James as the 'not a man move' shot. Alan Knott is the wicket-keeper

Square-cutting on the way to a century in a last appearance for West Indies at Lord's in 1973. Alan Knott and Raymond Illingworth follow the ball

Celebrating the West Indies' victory over England at the end of the 1973 Test

In the faster style ...

... and changing to spin

Left: An uninhibited slash over cover point, a risky but necessary shot as one-day cricket proliferated

Below: The game may have changed but the fundamentals have not

Above: Taking a place in the hall of fame

Left: Accompanying Brian Lara around the golf course, when advice could be sought and given in private

Above: Sir Gary and Brian Lara joined on the golf course by Ian Botham

Left: With Mike Procter, another great all-rounder, when South Africa returned to Test cricket

Above: Seeing for the first time the
enthusiasm for the game in Soweto

Right: The game has never lost its
appeal

The consultant to the Barbados Board of Tourism ponders upon his next task

game at an age when he still had a considerable amount to offer. It was not right that he should be picked and dropped on a whim. During my playing career I kept myself fit by swimming, running on the beach and playing tennis, basketball and football. For relaxation I played dominoes and, later in my career, golf, which I still play today. My friends know that if I am not watching cricket from the commentary position I can be found on the golf course or at a domino table.

A man who participates in top-class sport should know just how fit he needs to be to play at his peak. We all suffer from off days resulting from too much travel, cold weather – even in the English summer my overcoat is usually close at hand – or stomach trouble caused by strange food or impure water. Or possibly just a hangover! The great thing is to know your own body. Only you know what food suits you best and what you need most to enable you to relax. Those England players, including the captain, Graham Gooch, who ate prawns on the eve of a Test in India during their 1992–93 tour should have thought twice about doing so. This was not Southend-on-Sea.

Diet is important, too, although this can be taken to unnecessary extremes. Even now, years after retiring from the game, I am particular about what I eat. Unfortunately, growing up as I did in a region where so many citrus fruits were available has left me unable to eat them any longer. I have consumed too much acid through the years for the good of my stomach. Staying in hotels, as I do regularly around the world, has enabled me to be able to choose from a wide selection of dishes, but I have never much liked cold meals or rich fare dressed up under some high-falutin name. And you cannot call yourself a cricketer in England until you have eaten a ton of lettuce.

Modern-day cricketers travel so much that they literally live in hotels, and the diet is usually of a consistently high standard. They can save on their tour allowances by not going out of their hotels in search of some swish restaurant, although most cricketers enjoy Chinese and Indian cooking and will eat out at times in those restaurants. I was never a huge eater and neither my methods of energizing myself nor my particular physical exercises would benefit everybody.

Rather than lap the ground endlessly, or go in for what used to be called PT with an instructor or trainer, I had an inherent belief in abdominal exercises. These are often overlooked by cricketers. Working on one's stomach muscles coupled with some deep breathing is of immense value. When inhaling, the breath should be held for a few seconds before the stomach and abdomen muscles are pulled in, which helps to blow the air out of the lungs. It is a tip I can recommend to any aspiring or established player.

I expressed my view in *Cricket Crusader* more than 30 years ago that no other sport, except perhaps running a marathon, requires such physical effort as does cricket. This may sound strange when one considers how much exertion and constant movement go into a game of football, but it lasts for only 90 minutes. Cricket lasts all day. Indeed, given that matches now start earlier than they did and go on longer as a result of slow over-rates, the stamina and concentration required take a huge toll. Throw in night cricket and the requirements made of all fielders in the instant game and you can see the importance of a cricketer looking after his own well-being. If he is capable of playing for his country, he will know what sort of shape he should be in.

Fielding

Because of the demands of one-day cricket and the need for players to be on their toes at all times, there is a greater concentration today on fielding. One of the most significant improvements in the modern game has come about through the emphasis placed on this. Players today practise extensively under the watching eyes of the manager and coach, and the results are pleasing. About 80 per cent of all catches offered are taken, compared with about 50 per cent when I was playing. A specialist slip fielder was always adept in his "box" and there were always exceptional deep fielders with strong arms, but the all-round standard was raised only through the advent of one-day cricket. This has proved to be the greatest legacy of the instant game, apart, of course, from bringing more people through the turnstiles.

Much of the success of the West Indies in the last 20 years must be attributed to the outstanding slip cordon which backed up a succession of outstanding fast bowlers. They say "catches win matches" and Viv Richards, Gordon Greenidge, Clive Lloyd, Gus Logie, Richie Richardson, Desmond Haynes, Carl Hooper and Brian Lara prove the adage. In recent times Carl Hooper and Phil Simmons have emerged as outstanding close catchers; they have some of the safest pairs of hands I have ever seen.

Overs per hour

One of the aspects of the game that has changed dramatically from my playing days with the West Indies is the number of overs bowled per hour. In my day, with Lance Gibbs and myself bowling regularly, we used to get in 18–20 overs in an hour. When the great spin twins Sonny Ramadhin and Alf Valentine were in the team, the West Indies used to average 22–23 overs per hour some days. Yet these teams still possessed fast bowlers: Wes Hall and Charlie Griffith had lengthy run-ups and the likes of Roy Gilchrist and Chester Watson were not inclined to hurry through their overs.

When the West Indies switched to a four-prong pace attack with great success, it inevitably meant that fewer overs would be bowled per hour. The fact that this approach won Test matches meant that slower over-rates became the norm throughout international cricket. You cannot force a bowler to shorten his run, and when the ball has to be retrieved from the boundary, it is all part of the over. I don't know whether the authorities and critics ever take into calculation that in India a great number of maidens are bowled, hence speeding up the over-rate.

The International Cricket Council's stipulation that 90 overs must be bowled in a day, or otherwise fines are incurred, is fair enough. Whenever I consider this, I think back to the Trinidad Test against England in 1967–68, when England, deploying not fast bowlers but spinners, slowed the game down to 12 overs an hour. There was no criticism of Colin Cowdrey's tactics. I uttered my frustration on many occasions but no one paid any attention, other than Brian Close – who the previous summer had lost the England captaincy to Colin through slowing down a championship game when leading Yorkshire.

I believe, as a result of this, that there should be some kind of rule stipulating that an over should be bowled in so many minutes if the ball is not going to the boundary. I took the view that England's cricket in that series was not good for the game, which led to my making a much-criticized declaration and England winning the match in the last over. I remember trudging round to the press box afterwards and emphasizing that England's tactics were ruining the game and that the Test, like the previous ones in the series, would have ended in a dull stalemate had I not declared. Even our umpires played up to our opponents, for England players had told them how good they were. I would never want to slow up a game and never did. If my team was not good enough, I would not want to use delaying tactics.

Everyone is down on the bowlers, but what about slow batsmen? I remember talking to Ken Barrington and being told, "Gary, I used to score 40 runs in no time at all and I was dropped. If I made 40 runs in two hours, they would play me." There might have been the odd occasion when he and Geoff Boycott were dropped for slow scoring, but those sentiments

NO PLAY TODAY. WITH COLIN COWDREY, FRIEND AND OPPONENT
OF LONG-STANDING

were typical of how cricketers were bred in England – and elsewhere. Ken wore himself into the ground worrying about his game. In 1965 he took more than seven hours to make 137 against New Zealand, who were at the time far from a strong side. He was indeed left out of the team for the following Test, but on the grounds that England were supposed to play attractive cricket against such lowly opposition, a kind of flying-the-flag exercise. Trevor Bailey and even, on occasion, Godfrey Evans bored spectators rigid in the 1950s.

In the West Indies, we always had a different approach and our batsmen generally did not become so anxious about their game. Andy Ganteaume, the Trinidadian, played one Test against England in 1947 and was promptly dropped for slow scoring – for good.

The amazing thing was that Andy made a century in his one innings. But it took him $4\frac{1}{2}$ hours, and Gerry Gomez, his captain and also a Trinidadian, had to send out a note to tell him to score more quickly. In the next Test, John Goddard moved up the order from number eight to open the innings and Andy never played Test cricket again. In the context of West Indian cricket, this was very slow batting. Peter Lashley, who played in my era, batted in a similar vein but played in only four Tests. I cannot think of any batsman in the Caribbean who would have prospered merely through occupying the crease and who would consequently have irritated spectators and administrators by slowing down the game. Batsmen have as much to answer for as fast bowlers in this regard.

Impact of television

The televising of international cricket has had a major impact on the game. It has brought the cricketing countries of the world closer together and has greatly increased the game's popularity. I would argue that a whole new generation of cricketing enthusiasts has emerged in recent times because of televised cricket, in particular the television-addict housewife. I would not wish to wager a bet on how many meals were burnt when Ambrose was destroying England in Port-of-Spain and Lara was breaking my record in Antigua in 1994.

Perhaps, however, TV's greatest impact has been on the players, who can have matches taped from start to finish and replay the tapes to see their mistakes and weaknesses as well as those of their opponents. Replays of tapes can also assist captains in focussing on mistakes they may have made in field placings and where they have gone wrong in other areas. But there is also a bonus for ex-players. Whereas in England and Australia there have always been television commentators, a new industry has developed in the West Indies and the Indian sub-continent for retired players to share their knowledge and expertise as TV experts who can earn a reasonable living in their sunset years.

Granting television rights has also been a boon to cricket administrations and has put them in a position to pay players much better for their services. In addition, it has significantly augmented the funds available to countries to upgrade their playing facilities and sponsor youth tournaments. In 1994 televised cricket really hit the jackpot with the agreement between Sky TV and the Test and County Cricket Board for broadcast rights which were valued at $60 million.

Weight of bat

In my view, the authorities need to consider carefully whether it is in the best interests of the game to allow batsmen to use any bat they wish or whether there should be a limit placed on the weight of the bat. I have already said that changes in the rules of the game through the years have overwhelmingly been to the benefit of the batsman, and this is one example. Batsmen using the extra-heavy bats only have to push the ball using minimum force and it speeds away through the field to the boundary.

At the same time, in the wrong hands, the new make of "jumbo bats" can be a liability, severely handicapping some batsmen when they try to cope with short-pitched deliveries, whether trying to defend when the ball is skidding through at upper body level or when trying to play the hook or pull shots. I would like to see the International Cricket Council place a limit on the weight of bats in the same way that a limit has been put on the weight of balls.

Displays of emotion

The enthusiasm the modern player shows by clapping and shouting to his colleagues on the field acts as a morale-booster and lifts the team. It can look unedifying, especially if this occurs when a batsman plays a good-length ball back along the pitch off the middle of his bat. These attitudes came into the game with the growth of one-day cricket, the influence of football – a player like Denis Law would salute the fans with his arm aloft when he scored a goal in the 1960s – and less rigidity in the behaviour of players, especially in England. In the West Indies, we were more inclined to let our feelings show at the fall of an important wicket. We did not shout in the field, but that did not mean we were any less enthusiastic. Applauding a good ball is for the benefit of team spirit and helps to motivate the bowler.

I know that numerous players from my generation do not approve of shouting on the field of play. David Steele, the former England batsman, actively discouraged young cricketers from piping up until they had made their way in the game. To see third man appealing for an lbw decision does not do anything for the team other than to put unnecessary pressure on the umpire. But I do not feel that this has anything to do with whether the spectators like it or not. I do remember talking to Gordon Greenidge during the 1992 World Cup about fielders doing the "high fives". He had been omitted

from the tournament by the West Indies selectors – erroneously – and he said he felt that there was something amiss
because he did not see this form of celebration going on in the
field. Followers of West Indian cricket might have felt there
was some animosity among the players.

Sledging

What West Indian cricketers have not gone in for is "sledging",
the verbal abuse of a batsman that has become commonplace
in Australia, even in club cricket. I myself never sledged and
when it was done to me I was not affected. It has been going on
as a psychological ploy for many years and yet batsmen have
still been scoring runs. It used to be called gamesmanship; it is
just more widespread now and more widely discussed in the
media. Some of it does set a bad example, not least when animosity is shown and stumps are kicked as a result of bad feelings. But what can the umpires do about it?

The more attention that is paid to sledging, the more it will
happen. The media are trying to find a story by writing about
it, rather than writing for the benefit of the authorities. Everybody blames the increase in sledging on the Australians
because they play the game hard, but I saw one of the worst
examples at first hand when the West Indies played Surrey at
the Oval in 1957. They were a tough, successful team who rent
the air blue with their language. The Aussies do not pretend to
be diplomatic but there are others who try to upset batsmen in
a sly way which is not so readily noticed. At the start of my Test
career, the West Indies took defeats and walked off with a
smile. When we began to win, attitudes towards us changed.

I took the view years ago – and wrote as much – that there
was no point in playing cricket at half-cock. It reduces your
pleasure in the game and gives less value to any of the performances in it. You must play hard. This does not mean glower-
ing at your opponents, appealing for ridiculous decisions and

being bad-tempered. Far from it. You can be cheerful, light-hearted, sympathetic and courteous to both your team-mates and your opponents but this still does not prevent you from playing competitively.

New temptations and pressures

Bad behaviour, of course, has to be stamped out. Stumps were not erected to be kicked down and players should not bet against their own team, as Dennis Lillee and Rodney Marsh did in the third Test against England in 1981. England were in a hopeless position, so hopeless that the odds against them winning were put at 500 to 1 at a stage of the match when Australia were at 1 to 4 and a draw was quoted at 5 to 2. You can see the temptation in backing your opponents in those circumstances although there was a risk of bad publicity and of alienation with their team-mates. It was clearly not the right thing to do, but only serves to emphasize that the danger of falling for such temptation is ever-present. Both Dennis and Rodney were huge triers and would never have put in indifferent performances just to win some money.

I have always felt that what makes an honest man is reasoning with himself over whether or not he would give in to temptation. After all, Jesus was disowned by disciples who had told him they would stand by him. It is nonsense for us to say that Bradman (or any other great and scrupulous cricketer) would have played in the same spirit today as he did in his time, because we simply don't know. None of us can say how we would have reacted because the rewards and the incitement to wrongdoing were not there in our day, although I like to think that the money at stake would not have made any difference to the way I played the game. The incentive then in playing for your country was honour. Playing to win and playing fairly should still be the case but it has to be understood that cricket is no longer made up of Gentlemen and Players.

No longer does a great cricketer like Alan Knott have to go on the dole, now that there are tours every winter; and if there is a gap in the official programme, it is quickly filled by some money-making venture or other, or even a breakaway tour. In today's world it would not be possible to have any amateurs in the game because they would be away from their workplace so often that no one would offer them a job. The exception in the West Indies is Philo Wallace, who is making a living outside of cricket, but if he joined the pool of Test cricketers, he would have to turn professional.

Sadly, I am told there is not the same camaraderie among the players, either. The pressures and the changes in the game are breeding different attitudes. There is more cricket under the microscope, more incidents, more reaction. In the past, certain occurrences, such as Freddie Trueman snatching his hat from an umpire's hands at the end of an over in the West Indies, were not reported, partly because there were no television cameras present.

A degree of trust

Times might have changed, but there should still exist between cricketers a degree of trust. If a fielder claims a fair catch, then the batsman should respect his integrity. If that integrity is found to be wanting, then his captain should have no truck with such cheating. I recall becoming angry with Basil D'Oliveira when he did not accept Conrad Hunte's word that he had taken a catch fairly during a Test in England. Conrad, who at the time was involved with moral rearmament, is an honourable man who would never cheat anybody. Basil would have known of his reputation and should have left the crease. Another player from my era, the Australian batsman Brian Booth, would prefer, if there was any element of doubt, to say he had not caught the ball rather than for the batsman to be out. There may be more pressures, financial pressures at any rate, on the players now, but the ethics have not changed down the years. The game has to be played in the right spirit, as well as to the letter of the law.

Ratings in cricket

The concept of assessing cricketers through individual ratings and then promoting these ratings on television does not bear scrutiny. Ted Dexter is a man and a cricketer whom I greatly admire, but I am not a believer in his system of assessing Test cricketers because statistics are not always the right criteria for judging players. It amazes me that this can be given so much credence. Averages are a better guide but even they do not detail how often a bowler may have come up against tail-enders. I am also surprised how any team can call themselves world champions, for such judgements are not made on one match or even one series, like a boxing fight.

The most proper ratings are made by a cricketer's peers. Reputation is what counts. All the averages and all the ratings do not show that the greatest cricketers were the ones who dominated and destroyed bowlers, who made them bowl what they wanted. Ted Dexter played that way. So, too, did Sir Donald Bradman, Everton Weekes and Ian Chappell. Viv Richards could destroy an attack. Instead, these ratings tell you that David Gower is a great batsman and Ian Botham a great all-rounder. Why? Because they have scored a lot of runs or taken a lot of wickets. Every era has thrown up great players, and Ian and David would rank highly in their particular era, but would probably fall short when placed alongside the all-time greats.

English pitches

Pitches, as with grounds around the world, have altered dramatically since my playing days. I well remember talking to Sir Gubby Allen a few years ago and telling him that England were frightened of the West Indies and preparing flat pitches accordingly. They were attempting to take the sting out of the bowlers by preparing surfaces that would nullify the threat of Roberts, Holding, Marshall, Croft and so on. In other countries, conditions have changed through natural circumstances rather than through any ploy of an authority or groundsman.

I enjoyed coming to England in 1957 and playing in difficult conditions. On that tour, only Eastbourne and Trent Bridge did not have any grass left on. It was a great challenge to play on pitches on which the ball was constantly seaming around, and bowlers such as Tom Cartwright and Derek Shackleton, who both exploited this to the full, caused considerable problems. Bowlers today find their task much more difficult because they are not accustomed to these conditions. At times that summer so much grass had been left on that you could not tell the pitch from the square. The experience helped improve batting technique and made you a better player. From what I see and hear, there are few green tops remaining in England any more.

As a result, batsmen can get away with technical imperfections. When the Reader ball with its high seam became disused in England, bowlers began complaining in the early 1990s that its replacement had more in common with a tennis ball, of little use to seamers and spinners alike. There must be a balance between bat and ball if the game is to continue to be a fair contest. Balls without a proper seam, even if they were brought in to redress the balance between batsmen and moderate bowlers who were taking too many wickets, are ridiculous. The way for a batsman to improve his technique is to learn to play on pitches on which the ball is moving around.

Caribbean pitches

In the Caribbean, the pitches have become much slower. Kensington Oval in Barbados has deteriorated to the extent that the bounce is sometimes uneven and it is not possible for fast bowlers to generate the pace they once did. Nothing has changed scientifically there but the square is used much more now than was the case in the past and the groundsmen are not as good as they were. Guyana is unchanged, but Kingston, Jamaica, is currently improving. The square started to deteriorate during West Indies' series against England in 1967–68, when the surface began to crack up. It had previously been so shiny that you could see your face reflected and, when I was talking to Mark Waugh when Australia played there in 1994, he mentioned that the sheen had returned.

When England played us in 1967–68, the Sabina Park pitch was criss-crossed by wide cracks and was fiery and sporting. John Snow bowled magnificently against us, taking seven for 49 in our first innings, but when we followed on I managed to make an unbeaten century in more than six hours' batting. I always enjoyed batting at Kingston because the pitches were so quick. Indeed, it is my favourite ground.

Another way in which the game has changed there is the earlier starts, at either 10.00 or 10.30 rather than 11.00 or 11.30. Dew can form on the pitch just as it can in England, which means the ball will move around more at the start of the day's play.

Pitches of the sub-continent and Australia

On the sub-continent, conditions have changed considerably in 20 years. When I played in Pakistan, it was on matting. In India, Calcutta was a green top in my day. Now, the grass is taken off. I have not been to Madras since 1968 and Delhi, which is preferred to Bombay as a Test centre, seems to have altered as well.

In Australia, there have been so many changes to the square at Melbourne that everybody is concerned as to how it is going to play. It has been torn up and down in the past. The

Sydney Cricket Ground, always a sound playing surface in my day, has become flatter and flatter. Perth, the ground on which in 1971–72 Dennis Lillee was as frightening a proposition as any fast bowler I faced, became slower but is now, I gather, back to the fearsome quick track it was then.

The role of the administrator

There was a greater division between administrators and players in my day than is the case now. The age of player power, as it is known, effectively began with World Series Cricket, although the likes of Ian Chappell were starting to dictate to their Boards of Control – and making themselves thoroughly unpopular – even before then. It would have been unheard of when I began in the game for players to insist on receiving more money or declaring that such and such a hotel was beneath their presence. Administration was inflexible and the players were the servants of the game and of the Board itself. Most administrators, it should be added, were well-meaning and saw it as their duty to give of their services. Perhaps the inevitable upshot of this was that they were not in the vanguard of moves to do something about cricketers' pay.

I had one well-documented row with administrators, indeed with my own Board of Control and selectors in the Caribbean at the beginning of 1973. There was a difference of opinion over an issue that should have been resolved without any disagreement: my own fitness. It only goes to show just how easily a minor dispute can turn into a quite unnecessary row. I had played 87 consecutive Tests for the West Indies and should, I felt, have been able to decide for myself whether or not I would be fit to play against Ian Chappell's Australians. The Board, rather than taking me at my word that I would be fit for the second Test of that series, instead asked me to prove my fitness by playing for Barbados. As a former captain and a senior player, I felt they should not have questioned my judgement: they ought to have known I would not let them down. The upshot was that I did not play at all in that series, which was bad enough. What made it even worse was that my disagreement was with two former colleagues and long-standing friends, Clyde Walcott and Jeffrey Stollmeyer.

Nobody personified the well-meaning (and thoroughly knowledgeable) administrator more than Sir Gubby Allen. A bachelor and formerly a distinguished cricketer, he had his own key to the ground at Lord's from his house just behind the Warner stand. He lived for the game, was full of wisdom and had sufficient capital not to have to look to it for a living. He was the embodiment of the amateur who loves the sport and whose views are not questioned because of his venerability and wisdom. There were others like that, men like Sir Donald Bradman and Jeffrey Stollmeyer, who knew all there was to know about the game. Today, my old colleague and friend Sir Clyde Walcott has succeeded Colin Cowdrey as chairman of the ICC, and in his 70s has to do an immense amount of travelling and diplomatic negotiation. I admire him for it. There were also some administrators whose roles I could never quite fathom out.

Many difficulties and some criticisms of their roles arose through experiments and changes to the laws of the game. The front-foot rule, short-pitched bowling, throwing and the lbw law have all led to differences of opinion. I have mentioned already that it would have been best not to have tinkered with anything save for the ruling over the front foot. All that has resulted has been a good deal of controversy, a certain amount of negative cricket and the persecution of players such as Tony Lock and Charlie Griffith. I cannot see the attraction of becoming involved in any of these areas. I have long maintained that rather than messing about with the laws, fixture planning and suitable ground and playing comforts are of far greater importance.

NEARING THE END OF A LONG CAREER

The authorities all over the world were fortunate that cricketers have been, by and large, a conservative bunch. Had they been more militant, someone like Kerry Packer could have made an impact upon the game and the pay and conditions far sooner.

In England, the Cricketers Association, comprising all the first-class players, was a mild-mannered organization which had little in common with the powerful trade unions that existed there in the 1960s and 1970s. John Arlott's proudest achievement was to have become their president, for he empathized with the ordinary player and wished to see him prosper. The introduction of a minimum wage for a capped cricketer was a long time coming but there was no changing the realization that high earnings would be for only the best players.

Until 1967, cricketers were virtually the only group of workers in Britain who had no say in their own affairs or conditions of employment. The Cricketers Association, initially a penniless organization, operates through an annual meeting of all members, held in April, and, in day-to-day matters, through an executive and an elected representative from each county. Greatly to the credit of the Test and County Cricket Board, which was formed the following year, taking over the running of cricket from MCC, there was no gulf between the two bodies from the outset. They recognized the Cricketers Association's worth and its moderate voice even before some professional cricketers did.

This was administration at its best: a genuine desire to see the lot of the average cricketer improved, or at least kept on a reasonable financial footing. The only time I have known any hostility surface was at the time of World Series Cricket, when there were calls for action against players who had signed for Packer and who wanted to continue in county cricket, and when there was further concern over whether the World Cup in England in 1979 would be affected by the participation of those contracted to Packer.

106

The point is that no matter how many changes are made to the laws, to the administrative bodies and to the codes of conduct, the game will not become any more attractive to players or spectators if the playing conditions are not suitable. Decent cricket cannot be conjured up if either too much grass is left on the pitch to favour the seam bowlers or if it is so slow that the ball does not come onto the bat. The ideal pitch has a consistency of bounce, gives some help to the new-ball bowlers and favours the spinners as the match continues. This is so blindingly obvious that it should not have to be spelled out to any individual exercising power. Yet few administrators are seemingly aware that this should be their first priority. Too often in the past the host country has looked after itself when preparing a pitch for a Test match, which is self-defeating.

Sightscreens

Many of the players involved in world cricket today find it hard to believe just how basic some of the conditions were for Test matches, let alone county matches, in the past. It is astonishing to think now that there was no sightscreen at the pavilion end at Lord's when Colin Cowdrey had his arm broken by Wes Hall in 1963. The white seats were supposed to act as a suitable backdrop and yet they were filled with spectators. Even now, a number of grounds used for county cricket in England do not have proper sightscreens in place. Temporary edifices are put up which can comprise no more than a billowing piece of canvas without any steward in place to stop spectators moving across it. If cricketers are to travel miles for a tour or even an ordinary first-class fixture, it is imperative that they have suitable equipment provided for them to ply their trade.

Growing up in Barbados, in clear light and on pitches of consistent bounce, I did not need to pay too much attention to the backdrop to the bowler's arm. Kensington Oval, even when I was young, possessed a wide screen that did not have to be altered every time a bowler decided to go around the wicket. When I came to England, I discovered that all the smaller grounds understandably wanted to use up all their seating when there was a capacity crowd present. In those circumstances, the sightscreen sometimes had to be sacrificed to gain greater revenue.

There was no guarantee, either, that the sightscreen would be correctly stationed. The one in use at Old Trafford was too low. Even now, a bowler with a high arm such as Lance Gibbs or Joel Garner will deliver the ball from the seating above the sightscreen and hence is much more difficult to play. This is indeed an unfair advantage but one that is difficult to eradicate.

Light meters

Similarly, the introduction of light meters is an important addition to the game in an age when spectators are having to pay big money for watching a top match. Umpires can no longer expect crowds to accept dictatorial decisions based on their own eyesight or over-concern for the safety of the players. Dickie Bird, one of the finest of modern umpires, tells the story of officiating at a first-class match for the first time. It was a county match at the Oval and he was to be partnered by Cec Pepper, an uncompromising Australian. Dickie, who was a considerable fusspot himself when it came to deciding what to do in murky conditions, felt play was perfectly possible.

When he told Pepper what he felt, Dickie was told: "It's too bad and that's all there is to it." He tried to suggest a starting time and Pepper replied: "You suggest nothing. You sit there." Press enquiries as to why the start had been delayed were met with curt remarks. The umpire's decision was final – or at least it was until cushions started raining down on to the outfield from MCC members, of all people, when a re-start was not made to the Centenary Test at Lord's in 1980. By then, spectators were not prepared to tolerate an umpire's judgement when their own inclination told them that play was possible. The introduction of the light meter, especially the kind visible to all at grounds such as Old Trafford, was an important step forward. Now an umpire will know the precise moment at which he can offer the light to a batsman and hence not incur the wrath of any member or spectator.

Computerized scoring

We live in the computer age and it was inevitable, I suppose, that the days of the quill or fountain pen and rectangular book of parchment paper would not last for ever. It is sad to see them go, although some of the older scorers understandably cannot bring themselves to adopt new technology. I am told that the advent of computerized scoring results in a valuable database. I am also told that scorers were not given proper training upon the introduction of this in 1993 and that they were not paid properly, either, for coping with what amounted to considerable extra work.

Any mechanized system of scoring should still be supported by hand-written detail, for machines have a tendency to break down. No longer can the joke be made about the scorer falling asleep after a good lunch, for it is more likely to be the computer. Some of my old friends from the game who have turned to scoring rather than, say, umpiring, have experienced numerous difficulties in getting to grips with a system that is alien to them. Yet one benefit in a fast-moving world is that scores can be transmitted more quickly and accurately to the waiting world than was the case in the past. And that has to be good for the game.

CHAPTER 9

Innovations in Bowling

The West Indies under Lloyd was a team of several great players who would succeed in any company, but it is clear that West Indies cricket in recent times has blossomed because of the generally poor quality of the opposition. It is true that there have been some outstanding batsmen, but success has been built around successive quartets of fast bowlers of genuine world class, some bowling at express pace, others concentrating more on movement.

Intimidatory bowling

Malcolm Marshall, Mike Holding, Andy Roberts, Joel Garner, Colin Croft, Curtly Ambrose, Ian Bishop and Patrick Patterson tormented all batsmen and guaranteed West Indies dominance for almost 20 years. They exposed the flaws of batsmen who seemed quite incapable of playing pace and many of whom, on account of poor techniques, had not mastered the swinging ball.

I wrote when I was a player that no captain tolerates intimidating bowling. But there are always two sides to the difficulties posed by a truly fast bowler. The majority of opening batsmen, at least in the days when techniques were more sound than they are now, would combat him skilfully enough.

Two might be hit and conceivably break a bone. Such an incident unfortunately causes more comment than everything else in the match put together, even if some of the other batsmen have scored freely off the same bowler. Sometimes the pitch causes the ball to fly off a length. Sometimes the ball skids through after becoming wet on a damp outfield. Possibly the batsman has just come to the wicket and has not attuned himself to the glare or a drizzle or the line of flight. When I captained teams in first-class cricket, I would tell a batsman waiting to go in to sit outside and become accustomed to the light. Now, some players counter bright sunlight by wearing sunglasses. Although they are mainly fielders, I recall Gordon Greenidge batting in sunglasses at times. Some of these players obviously do so for advertising reasons. I personally would not have wanted to wear a pair for cricketing reasons and don't know of any cricketer who has suffered skin cancer or cancer of the eye through not properly protecting himself.

The great Frank Worrell caused some upset when he was captain of West Indies by not allowing card playing during stoppages for rain and, indeed, card playing in the evening, unless there was a rest day starting the following morning. He reasoned that this resulted in eye strain, which affected his team once they returned to the middle. He had made a study of optics, the science of light and vision, and decided that a batsman could be mistiming strokes through having played his hand in poor light. When one considers how often a batsman's wicket goes down upon resumption after a break in play, his argument evidently had some validity. We switched, instead, to playing table tennis, which sharpened the reflexes and kept the eye in.

But this is to digress. A batsman who cannot avoid the short-pitched ball might simply find that his reflexes are not what they once were. He could also be in difficulty through a poorly positioned sightscreen, a dark background – batsmen reckoned that Joel Garner's height was such that the ball came out of the row of seats above the sightscreen and hence was much more difficult to pick up – a distraction caused by a passing bird or a bit of litter whipped up by the wind, or simply a basic lack of concentration. All these are reasons for misjudging a quick delivery and being hit by it.

Of course sympathy should be shown to the poor batsman who is hit, even if through his own failings. But if a batsman comes to the crease and clearly cannot handle bouncers, it is within the fast bowler's right to bowl them. Although in my time I hardly ever saw one fast bowler bowl a bouncer at another, just because someone comes in at number nine or ten does not mean he can't bat. As soon as a bowler has a weapon, some onlookers feel he should not be allowed to use it. But cricket was not intended to be a game for batsmen to dominate.

If the game is made too easy for a batsman, then it simply becomes too one-sided. As it is, the pitches have become a lot slower than they used to be, which makes a bowler's life even harder. Neither is he taking part in a match to act as cannon-fodder. This is not to say there have not been times when a bowler overdoes the bouncer by delivering a ball that flies four feet over the batsman's head. It should be used as a weapon to keep the batsman guessing: I attempted to bowl it as quickly as Wes Hall did, in other words considerably faster than my stock delivery.

I do not go along with the view that when I played in the 1950s, 1960s and 1970s, there were fewer bouncers. Batsmen then could hook better than they can today. Nobody said Fred Trueman could not bowl two bouncers to one batsman in an over, which the International Cricket Council would not have allowed him to do throughout his career had he played two decades later than he did. I remember Ray Lindwall and Keith Miller coming to the Caribbean in 1954–55 and peppering batsmen with bouncers. No one said anything about it. I remember Peter Pollock bowling a great many bouncers at tailenders when he played for South Africa. Again, there was

no adverse reaction. What has happened subsequently is that West Indies' four-prong attack has made everybody focus on the issue.

I always looked to try to hook the short-pitched ball. If a batsman prefers not to hook, fair enough. But he must master the art of swaying out of the line, an art that sadly sometimes has been neglected since the introduction of helmets. It is vital to watch the ball until the last possible moment, keeping the head as still as possible. A batsman who is not capable of getting out of the way of the short-pitched ball should not be playing in the first place.

Penalizing fast bowlers

I have never believed in changing the laws of the game for the benefit of batsman or bowler. When the ruling restricting to two the number of fielders behind square was brought into effect, limitations were placed on the in-swing bowler. He was no longer able to attack the batsman with three leg-slips and I do not see how that can be construed as fair. Nobody has ever made a rule to say that a batsman cannot hit five fours in one over. The only change of rule to help the poor old bowler is the one that makes it possible for a batsman padding up outside off-stump to be lbw to the ball coming back into him.

So I cannot go along with the idea that the West Indies should be penalized for possessing genuinely quick bowlers. Other countries, given the chance, would have played four fast bowlers of such quality. However, if the West Indies are to maintain their dominant position in world cricket, they must either find a combination of good spinners or a minimum of two fast bowlers of express pace. Looking at the Red Stripe series, the usual incubator for future Test players, I do not see many such fast bowlers around.

In addition to losing players through retirement or because of diminishing returns brought on by age there is the injury factor. A back injury has given Bishop numerous problems and makes his long-term future look doubtful. A shoulder injury forced Ambrose out of the 1993 Indian tour and could shorten his career. These are two very fine fast bowlers, Ambrose one of the greatest of his or any other time.

It is not difficult to predict that in future the West Indies will find that they will have to work harder to win Test matches unless they either find suitable replacements or come up with a new formula to replace the four-prong all-pace attack. But all may not be lost for them as some people are saying. If opposing teams do not lift the level of their game significantly, I can still see the West Indies continuing to dominate world cricket because of the emerging strength of their batting. This will be centred around Lara, Campbell, Adams and Chanderpaul.

Other Test teams

Looking around at the other Test teams, there does not seem to be any team superior to West Indies, in spite of Australia's notable victory in the Caribbean in 1995. India will do well in India but will find it more difficult in the West Indies. Pakistan, who I consider to have a good all-round team and who I thought would provide the most serious opposition to West Indies, have proved to be inconsistent.

The Australians looked as if they were on their way back when the West Indies toured in 1993–94. They started very well but they seemed to lose their way and their efforts eventually petered out. After Lara established his dominance they seemed to suffer a psychological decline and were never able to raise the standard of their game to the level reached during the first half of the tour.

The two Pakistani fast bowlers, Waqar and Wasim, whom I have mentioned already, were very disappointing when they came to the Caribbean. They bowled too short and too wide and seldom troubled the batsmen. They often seemed to be trying too hard and their length and direction suffered. Their failure to perform in accordance with their great reputations put additional pressure on their own batsmen and disappointed both West Indian spectators and their own supporters.

I had been watching Waqar and Wasim since 1990 and in my opinion they were two excellent bowlers of genuine pace who got significant movement and had fully deserved their international reputation as a formidable opening pair. However, I must express my disappointment at allegations which surfaced subsequently about ball tampering.

Ball tampering

There are many more complaints about ball tampering today than in the past, when these were few and far between. There has always existed the picking of the seam with fingernails and polishing one side of the ball using sun-cream or vaseline and perspiration to give the bowler an added advantage. As a result, administrators have put a stop to practices such as seam-lifting, the use of lip salve and batsmen roughing up the pitch with their spikes for their own spinners. But it should be stressed that such goings-on have never been as widely condemned as the behaviour of the batsman who refuses to walk or the slip fielder who picks up a catch on the bounce. One or two batsmen whom I played against established a reputation for walking when they edged a catch to the wicket-keeper. There were times when they did not live up to that reputation and yet still foxed the umpire, who reasoned that if they did not walk, they were evidently not out. It is one thing to leave the crease in a county match to an obvious snick and another to return to the pavilion when in the mid-90s during a Test match.

In my day, nobody complained if the ball was fiddled with. Nor did they complain when the ball was rubbed on the ground to remove the shine so that the spinners could be brought on early in the innings. The Indians, with outstanding spinners in their side like Bedi, Venkataraghavan, Chandrasekhar and Prasanna, and anxious to bring them into the attack, often took the shine off in that way.

It was acceptable that fast bowlers would polish one side of the ball to obtain extra movement. Every fast or medium-paced bowler did it. This was par for the course. But we relied on natural ability rather than artificial aids of any kind. We played the game the way I have always felt it should be played. The teams in which I played never cheated – they abhorred cheating. So when I heard that Imran Khan had used a bottle top to gouge the side of a ball, I could not believe it. I was not shocked because I did not think it was true – until I realized he had admitted this himself. Then I was surprised. I don't know whether to put this down to increasing strain on players to produce results, or if there is too much cricket played and they feel they have to win at all costs.

Now that ball-tampering has received so much adverse publicity, I am sure that television cameras and commentators will soon pick up on anything untoward going on. This was shown to be the case when the cameras homed in on Greg Matthews during the third Test between South Africa and England at Durban in 1995. My old colleague Clive Lloyd was the match referee and he decided that the bowler was above suspicion. The drawback now is that every cameraman and producer – and some commentators – will be over-zealous in their attempts to spot anything untoward. Also, any false movement by a fast bowler or fielder will draw the attention of the umpires. Certainly in my day I never heard of a fielder or 12th man bringing an implement onto the field to scar a ball. The same applies to a player having dirt in his pocket, as the England captain, Mike Atherton, had in order, he said, to dry his fingers during the Lord's Test in 1994. To me this was strange, for I never liked to wear soiled clothes, particularly not on a hot day. I never saw any cricketer put his hand in his pocket unless it was cold or he wanted to take out his handkerchief. The point is that nobody will do this again because the television cameras will be closing in on them as they did on Atherton. This again illustrates the increasingly useful role that television plays.

Because I always believed in giving the player the benefit of the doubt and not relying on hearsay, I was likewise sceptical when I heard the allegations of ball-tampering against the Pakistanis that were made by Allan Lamb in 1992. What caused suspicion was that a ball was changed during a one-day international that summer by the match referee – my old team-mate Deryck Murray – without any explanation. That and the subsequent admission of ball-tampering by Imran did not help Pakistan's cause. The newspaper allegations by Lamb cost him his England place and would have been virtually impossible to prove, anyway, for neither the International Cricket Council nor the Test and County Cricket Board would ever support him in public or in private on this matter. On the other occasions when the umpires or match referees examined the ball during play or in an interval in a one-day or Test match, they found nothing to complain about.

In that particular match between England and the Pakistanis at Lord's, Lamb had picked the ball up and shown it to the umpire, Ken Palmer, just before lunch. Lamb reckoned that one side was shiny and the other had been interfered with. What was not in doubt was that the Pakistanis were making an old ball swing more than they were a brand new one. It would swing in late in the banana-shaped curve known as reverse swing, which I mentioned in the previous chapter.

CHAPTER 10

Comparing All-Rounders

As an all-rounder, I am often asked about my successors in the game, how they compared with me and how the role has changed over the years. Comparisons will always be subjective and influenced by knowledge, friendship, partisanship or simply an individual having had the luck to be at a particular ground when a certain player has performed well. In these days of satellite television and enhanced terrestrial coverage, there is more footage of matches and individuals and hence more opportunity to pass judgement on the modern player.

It was, for instance, only through luck that the television cameras were rolling when I struck my six sixes at Swansea against Glamorgan in 1968. The coverage on Welsh television had finished for the day, even though a declaration was imminent and we were at a crucial stage of the match. The producer, sensing at the start of the over that history could yet be made, wisely left the cameraman in place, and the footage and Wilf Wooller's commentary are now an important part of the game's history. Numerous viewers, some of whom might not have seen me in action before, will have watched that. Yet there could so easily have been no coverage at all.

The exceptional all-rounders since I retired have all been fast or fast–medium bowlers and hard-hitting batsmen. This in itself has reflected the changing face of cricket, for the game in the 1970s and 1980s was dominated by fast bowling and powerful stroke-makers. An all-rounder like, say, Richie Benaud, would not have flourished to the same extent that he did in the 1950s and 1960s because he would probably not have been given the same opportunity to succeed. Spinners and particularly leg-spinners were not such a force in the game. This was partly because one-day cricket took an inexorable grip and partly because captains such as Clive Lloyd, Viv Richards and Ian Botham took the view that the quicks won matches and Test series.

I am delighted to see the resurgence of the spinner in the 1990s. For too many years bowlers – and not just those in the Caribbean – have attempted to bowl fast because it was associated with power and winning matches. Even an all-rounder whose place in the team was more or less assured through his batting would not look to bowl spin when he could reckon to work his way through the opposition with pace.

Tony Greig produced his best Test match figures, 13 wickets for 156, against the West Indies at Port of Spain in 1973–74, through bowling off-cutters and gaining notable bounce from his great height. It was a considerable feat against a strong batting line-up, yet when did he opt for that style again? On the grassy pitches in England or the hard surfaces in Australia, he reckoned he would have greater success in his faster mode. We remember him as a tall, gangly medium-pacer, but he could well have been more than a one-match wonder with his off-cutters.

Another all-rounder who had the potential for developing his slower style was Bernard Julien, with whom I shared a large partnership in my last Test at Lord's in 1973. But he, too, was mostly used as an opening bowler who could make the ball swing considerably, even though once Lance Gibbs retired there was the opportunity for him to bowl spin. His place in the team should have been assured through his all-round abilities and yet his career fell away to such an extent that he gave up county cricket, lost his Test place and ended up on a break-away tour of South Africa. There was no way back after that and now he cuts a sad figure in his native Trinidad.

Curiously enough, when I retired in 1974, there was no exceptional all-rounder in the game. Tony Greig, as I have mentioned, was a very good cricketer, then probably the best all-rounder to have played for England since Trevor Bailey; and Intikhab Alam, then captaining Pakistan, was a fine leg-spinner who could make useful runs. Keith Boyce, who delivered some quick spells during that 1973 series against England, was from my own island of Barbados and was exciting to watch. He would have been the ideal cricketer for the Rothmans Cavaliers. But none of these could be described as truly world-class.

Ian Botham

In the same year that I retired, a young man came to prominence in England for continuing to bat after having two teeth knocked out by Andy Roberts in a Benson and Hedges Cup tie. Ian Botham has rarely been out of the limelight since. I am often asked, particularly when I am travelling around the world, how good a cricketer he was and whether he was the best all-rounder I have seen. I have to say that I do not think he was a great player, a description which is tossed around all too lightly inside and outside the game. A very good player, yes, who could have become a great one. But he didn't.

Ian did something for English cricket at a time when it was in the doldrums, namely, bringing people back to the game – to watch it, play it, enthuse about it. His centuries against Australia in 1981 were tremendous innings which effectively won the Ashes and made him into a hero.

As a young bowler, before he developed back trouble, he possessed a fine away-swinger which helped enable him to take 100 wickets as well as make 1000 runs in his first 21 Tests, but a great number of these were against opponents weakened by the loss of their best players to World Series Cricket. Such feats in an era of unprecedented cult status unfortunately blinded others to his failings. He had a lot of ability but if he had had a more serious manner rather than a happy-go-lucky approach, he could have achieved more.

He paid little heed to his fitness, which meant his back suffered further undue strain and he was unable to move the ball away from the right-hander once he started to put on weight in his late 20s. He then began to believe every batsman was susceptible to the short ball and bowled far too many. Some of these may have resulted in catches at long leg or deep square, but he conceded too many runs in the process. If the true test of a top-class cricketer is how he performs under pressure against the strongest opposition, then Ian was found wanting. He enjoyed success against the Australians, who in 1979–80 had their World Series players back and who in 1981, even though their batting was weak, had Dennis Lillee and Terry Alderman to open their attack.

But Ian's batting against the strongest opponents of all – the West Indies – does not make for good reading. In 38 innings his highest score was 81 and his batting average only 21. In 20 Tests against them he took 61 wickets. He had a perfectly sound technique and stood up well against pace, so he really ought to have performed better than that with the bat. But this was in an era when England were over-run by strong West Indian teams and could come up with scant response to all-out pace and quick-scoring batsmen. For all that, Ian would still rank high, and perhaps above Imran Khan, Richard Hadlee and Kapil Dev as the great players of *that* era. If Ian had applied his talents, he could perhaps have ranked with the all-time greats.

Imran Khan

Pakistan through the years always had good batsmen and possessed one of the best balanced teams, including players like

Sarfraz, Intikhab, Imran Khan and Abdul Qadir. They always seemed to go in for a varied attack, unlike the West Indies, who played four quicks, and India who sometimes played four spinners. Imran was an excellent all-rounder and is clearly the Pakistani superstar of post-war cricket. As a batsmen he scored many runs in crucial situations. He was also an extremely good bowler who at the height of his career worked up more than useful pace. He was always very competitive, whether at county, one day or Test level. Greatness comes from natural ability and great players are expected to use their ability to reach the pinnacle of greatness. It is a major pity that Imran's reputation as a bowler has been tarnished by his own admission of ball-tampering, and the subsequent legal wrangling between him and Ian Botham is unedifying and bad for the game.

Imran gave great service to Pakistan as captain. He knew the game well and was an excellent leader of men. He gained the deepest respect and adoration of his players, who respected him as much for his fine cricketing mind as for who he was socially and culturally. Once he had made his mark, he bestrode all Pakistan teams, in which he played like a colossus. One of the hardest things for any captain is to get the players behind him, especially if there are one or two who might think that they should be captain. When the team is winning, the players will subsume their feelings, but when they are losing and things seem to be falling apart, and there is pressure from the media and public with everyone looking for a scapegoat, then the captain can tell who is fully backing him.

Imran's achievements as a captain were all the more impressive since the Pakistanis have proved so difficult to handle in recent years. It is said that you need a degree in insider dealing to cope with the machinations in their internal affairs and I have to say that I am as baffled as anybody over what has been going on in recent years. What I could understand, however, was the reaction of some of their senior players when Pakistan won the World Cup in Melbourne in 1992. It was a team effort and should have been rewarded as such. Yet in his speech at the post-match ceremony, Imran dedicated the victory – and hence, it was understood (erroneously), the financial rewards – to his cancer hospital project in Lahore, and did not mention the players. He was so intent on furthering his cause that he treated this triumph as if he had won a single-wicket competition. Apart from Javed Miandad, the other players were not as well off as Imran and understandably wanted to keep their prize money and any gifts showered upon them when they returned home. I do not think this amounted to greed, although they might have expressed their feelings in the wrong way. Most Pakistani cricketers come from impoverished backgrounds and cricket is all too short a career.

Nonetheless, although some of his players accused him of swearing at them on the field, Imran always seemed to retain his dignity and self-belief. One notable difference between him and Ian Botham was that he always kept himself in peak physical condition, did not drink and overcame a serious shin injury at a time when he was a really quick bowler. Yet his social activities were even more exacting than Ian's!

His strengths as a bowler, namely the ability to move the ball both ways at pace, and the self-discipline he acquired as a batsman that came with increasing maturity and being made captain at a time when it was reckoned fast bowlers could not make successful captains, were down to his own perseverance. He made the most of World Series and the knowledge of the cricketers he encountered. What was also particularly noticeable was that he sometimes opted not to play against the weaker opponents, preferring, instead, to take on the West Indies in the Caribbean while pushing himself as hard as he physically could. No wonder his team-mates looked up to him. Pakistan's cricket has not been the same since. In the 40 Tests Imran played when he did not lead Pakistan, he averaged 25.44 with the bat and took 175 wickets at 25.53 apiece. In his 48 matches

124

as captain, he averaged 52.34 with the bat and gained 187 wickets at the superior strike rate of 20.26. Considering he was not appointed captain until he was 29 and thus theoretically was past his best as a fast bowler, these are remarkable figures. His adherence to fitness meant that he became an even better cricketer at an age when the likes of Botham were in decline.

Kapil Dev

The two other all-rounders who completed a wonderful quartet in this period were Kapil Dev and Richard (now Sir Richard) Hadlee. Both had to lead their country's attacks more or less on their own, Kapil on pitches that were often unresponsive and Richard in a team that could never be described as a strong one.

Kapil played in a great many more Tests than the other three – 131 compared with Botham (102), Imran (88), and Hadlee (86). Hence his achievements should be better than theirs. Indeed they are: he took 434 Test wickets and made 5248 runs. He saw himself primarily as a bowler. In his youth he was capable of gaining the same late outswing as Botham and he struck the ball with vigour throughout his career. Acquiring more Test wickets than anybody else may well have been his greatest achievement, although the most memorable could well have been leading India to victory in the World Cup in 1983 over a powerful West Indies team who played poorly on the day. Nevertheless, partly because they were more effective bowlers throughout their careers, Imran and Hadlee are generally regarded as having been greater performers.

I think this is a fair summation. Kapil's bowling declined when he was in his 30s, not because he did not look after himself – he did – but probably as a result of having been overbowled when he was young. Like Hadlee, he had to carry his country's pace attack for a good many years and that inevitably took its toll, as, indeed, would the bland pitches. He had to work harder for his wickets in that he was used more as a stock bowler than a strike bowler, which said much for his enthusiasm. He grew up in a land dominated by spin bowlers and had to learn how to swing the ball – both ways – move it off the seam and develop a passable slower delivery. His captaincy during the 1983 World Cup was sufficiently impressive for India to win the trophy. They only had a total of 183 to defend in the final and yet made a tremendous fist of it. That Kapil did not retain the captaincy until he retired had more to do with the kind of intrigue that bedevils the game on the subcontinent than his own failings.

Kapil played one extraordinary innings during that 1983 World Cup which will for ever have a place in the great feats of one-day cricket. He went to the pitch, a damp one, at Tunbridge Wells with his team's total standing – or rather, tottering – at 17 for five. The opposition were Zimbabwe, who were not, then, on the Test circuit. Kapil proceeded to play what he termed "the innings of a lifetime" in making an unbeaten 175. India won the match and, after that, deserved to win the World Cup. Although naturally I wanted the West Indies to triumph in the final, this would have been their third successive victory in the competition and it was good for the game that another country was victorious.

Sir Richard Hadlee

Richard Hadlee was a different type of cricketer in that he made himself, through remarkable will-power, become the most analytical and probing of bowlers, one capable of putting ball after ball six inches outside off-stump, fractionally short of a length and not giving the batsman any inkling of which way it was going to move. He began as a coltish tearaway in New Zealand and, through playing day-in, day-out county cricket with my old team, Nottinghamshire, turned himself into one of the finest medium-pacers ever to grace the game.

126

Of this quartet, who between them scored 17,379 runs and took 1610 wickets in Test cricket, Hadlee is the all-rounder I most admire. That is partly because he made the most of his ability but also because he was always in control of what he was doing and of the game, which should be the case with the very best cricketers. He particularly proved himself by taking many of his 431 wickets away from his homeland. He could bowl opposing batsmen out on all surfaces and of how many bowlers can that be said? I am told he had an accountant's brain, that even at the bar he never stopped thinking about how many wickets he was going to take the next day. To my mind, such dedication is entirely laudable. Great cricketers still have to think about the game and work at improving themselves, preferably in the middle rather than in the nets.

It is interesting to note that Richard was the only one of the four not to lead his country, which made good sense. He could concentrate on his own game without any distractions. Derek Underwood once asked in a bemused way why so many cricketers wanted to become captains of their teams and you come to appreciate that he had a good point.

Richard's batting was not especially effective until the advent of World Series Cricket. The introduction of the helmet certainly assisted his game – although I cannot imagine too many bowlers were intent on bowling him bouncers for fear they would be given plenty back! He was a bold, clean hitter in the lower middle order who could transform a match, particularly a one-day match, in a jiffy. He was a player for his time, not so cavalier as Keith Miller, the greatest all-rounder of my time but one who might well have become bored with constant instant cricket. I judge a great player on the quality of the opposition rather than on how many runs and wickets he gains, for there has been so much more Test cricket played since the two years of World Series than there was before. Hadlee's achievements overseas, particularly in Australia and

England, make him worthy of a higher ranking than the three other all-rounders of his time. Figures support this in that he took his wickets at 22.29 apiece, including five in an innings 36 times. That is a more considerable record than the number of wickets he finished with.

Brian McMillan

The great joy about being an all-rounder is that you can always be in the game. An opening batsman who is out to the first ball of the match can spend the next two days in the pavilion. But if you can bowl, you always have something to look forward to and a chance of atoning for a low score. If I was out cheaply, at least I had more energy left for taking the new ball. The increased amount of one-day cricket played all around the world has made it imperative for a specialist to be able to contribute in other areas of the game. The ideal all-rounder in the game today is Brian McMillan of South Africa, who makes consistent runs in the middle order, is always attacking the batsman when he comes on first change and who takes sharp catches at slip. He is an aggressive cricketer, which helps, because cricket in the 1990s is an aggressive sport.

Now that the likes of Botham and Hadlee have retired, a cricketer such as McMillan becomes even more valuable. Decent all-rounders are at a premium and hence he can name his price when an English county comes in for him. Above all, I admire the all-rounder who plays with a sense of style – in the mould of Keith Miller – and I would encourage any youngster who has ability with both the bat and the ball to try to develop his expertise at both. But be sure to recognize which of these skills is likely to bring greater success. I always felt that I was better known for my batting; Richard Hadlee would say that he was more prominent as a bowler than as a batsman. Always remember that the all-rounder has more fun than any other player in the team.

CHAPTER 11

Brian Lara

I have a very special affection for Brian Lara, whose record-breaking career is only in its infancy and whose achievements in 1994 caught the imagination of cricket lovers everywhere. It is not just his ability as a batsman which has astounded me but also the fact that, in spite of his problems in 1995, he remains unspoilt by success. That is a rarity in international sport today. I regard him as a sportsman and a gentleman.

Record-breaking performances

Lara is the greatest batsman the world has seen since Viv Richards; Viv himself will tell you that Brian is the more gifted of the two. Lest we forget, in the space of three months in 1994 he had broken my record of the highest Test score when he made 375 in Antigua on 18 April against England. He followed that up on 6 June by scoring 501 not out for Warwickshire against Durham in a county match in England to record the highest-ever first-class score.

To have made those record-breaking scores at the age of 25 will impose tremendous pressure on him for the remainder of his career. Indeed, it has already done so. This is a great psychological challenge in itself since he has to perform at a level set by himself. Looking around at other Test players, it is difficult to see any other contemporary batsman even getting close to reaching it. I understand very well the challenge and the pressure. When I scored 365 not out against Pakistan in 1958 it was my first score over 100 and for the remainder of my career it was the elusive goal I was always chasing, but would never achieve. What Lara also has to contend with now is more intense concentration from the media, which has proliferated considerably over four decades.

Let me say, however, that Brian has one significant factor in his favour. Whereas I was selected as a bowler and was transformed into a batsman and a genuine all-rounder as the years rolled by, Lara was selected as a batsman and will always be first and foremost a batsman. He can therefore focus all of his energies in a single-minded way on his batting. It is unlikely that he will ever have to open the bowling for the West Indies or hold up one end for 20 overs or bowl 25 overs of spin. It could be argued that he has fewer opportunities to succeed; but equally, he has less chance of becoming enervated.

I told Lara well before he wanted to leave England in the middle of the West Indies tour in 1995 that he must make up his mind whether he wanted to make as much money as quickly as possible or whether he wished to remain at the top level of Test cricket for as long as possible. I also told him that county cricket was, in my view, not the best foundation on which to build a Test career.

Typically, after I had told him that, he went on to set new standards in county cricket and rewrite the record books, climaxing with his epic unbeaten 501. For the first time in the history of organized first-class cricket a batsman scored more than 500 runs in one innings. There is no doubting, though, that his decision not to return to Warwickshire for another season of county cricket in 1996 was a sensible one. He was evidently exhausted during and after the West Indies tour of England in 1995, which he said he did not enjoy on account of the behaviour, in-fighting and petty jealousies within the party.

130

BRIAN LARA HAS BEATEN SIR GARY'S RECORD TEST SCORE....

...AND RECEIVES APPROPRIATE CONGRATULATIONS

THE OPENING BOWLER. BOWLING TO RON HEADLEY, OF
WORCESTERSHIRE AND THE WEST INDIES, IN 1966

I was saddened to learn that he had been fined ten per cent of his tour fee for apparently going absent without permission and sadder still that he felt he had to drop out of the subsequent visit to Australia. He had just batted extremely well in Sharjah but clearly could not face the thought of any further one-day cricket, even though the World Cup was looming. His actions inevitably cost him money: one estimate put his potential loss of earnings at £500,000.

There was apparently a breakdown in communications with Peter Short, the President of the West Indies Board and a diligent man whom I know well. Brian reckoned that after Peter had talked him into staying with the tour party in England, no action would be taken against him by the Board. But he was subsequently fined for "absenting himself from the team and thus not making his services available for the duration of the tour". Brian wrote a letter of apology to the Board, renewing his commitment to West Indies cricket. He was subsequently told he would not be punished further for withdrawing from the tour to Australia, since no contractual arrangements were in place between him and the Board.

Everybody seemed to have a view on his behaviour, Michael Holding going so far as to suggest that he should "grow up". No doubt there has been some jealousy towards him from other players within the team, for he has broken more records and earned more money than anybody still in the game. I myself feel the root cause of the problem was that the Board allowed him to go home to conduct some business in the middle of the tour. That kind of tolerance inevitably breeds resentment, even if there was a gap in the fixture list.

Commercial aspects

There is an additional concern. What was his agent's role in all this? I understand Warwickshire were not too happy at his having his career mapped out, sometimes in ways beyond their control. Agents have changed a great deal since the days when Bagenal Harvey, whom I have mentioned with regard to his role with Rothman's Cavaliers, took charge of Denis Compton's chaotic affairs and turned him into "the Brylcream boy". Bagenal removed the chaos from his life and turned his client into Denis Compton Ltd – a prosperous business concern. (He had to begin by sorting out two trunkloads of papers, bills and uncashed cheques!) There was never any conflict with his playing career.

Somehow, though, the idea of a cricketer making money through advertising was not considered right and proper even in the 1960s and 1970s. I remember some adverse reaction when Colin Cowdrey was paid to smoke a cigar at a time when footballers were being turned into male models. This was somehow not quite cricket. All that has changed now, but the question remains whether what the cricketer does off the pitch clashes with what he does on it. And it was unedifying to see a difference of opinion between Lara's agent in London and the West Indies Board over whether or not Lara was allowed to miss the tour to Australia.

Advice from, and about, agents

There are obviously more agents in existence now because cricket has become a business. They should be used as a protective shield by the player who does not want to become involved in going into the details of a business transaction. Cricketers generally do not like to be seen turning other people down. Agents should be looking for ways to enrich their clients – but they tend not to when their client is already in the limelight. Then the player goes through a lean patch, is dropped by his country or simply can no longer cut the mustard – the agent cannot come up with any contracts and disappears. A 20-year old should not be taken in by an agent because he should be able to obtain advice from senior players. In the same way that

134

an agent advises a player, a player should be advised about an agent. The point is that a cricketer such as Brian cannot do too much business or undertake any endorsements because if his cricket is affected he won't receive any offers. He no longer has a commercial value.

Coping with pressure

Brian's approach to the game is such that he seemed to set himself a standard and kept telling himself that any score below 100 was a failure. His achievements in 1994 are phenomenal and bear recording here, thanks to Tony Cozier's "Caribbean Cricket Quarterly". Having set such very high standards, the pressure will be on him to maintain these standards and both towards the end of the English county championship season in 1994 and during the subsequent tour to India, I got the impression that the pressure was beginning to tell. Sadly, that did indeed prove to be the case.

Strange to say now, there was another, more gifted West Indian batsman than Lara to emerge in recent years. Lawrence Rowe had more potential and was more graceful in his movement. He also got behind the ball better and, of course, had a far better start to his Test career than Lara, making 300 runs over two innings on his debut for the West Indies against New Zealand in 1971–72, and following that with a triple century against England. But Brian is a very special player who works hard at his game, is a good thinker and has a good technique. The real change came during the 1993 Australian tour when he realized that to keep his place in the team and get to the top he needed more than just a quick 40, 50 or 60 and in his own interest and that of the team he needed to buckle down and score heavily.

I was in Canada when I heard that Brian had pulled out of the trip to Australia in 1995 because of unstated reasons at the time. The fact that he was later fined was not the whole reason for his withdrawal but it was certainly a contributing factor. I thought then that the Board would do everything they could to get him back in the team – as was subsequently shown when he was included in the squad for the World Cup. What did occur before the start of the competition was that Peter Short asked me to address all the players on behalf of the Board, to try to boost their morale and to act as a unifying force. I was not sure what effect this would have on the experienced players, who should not have been in need of guidance, but I was, of course, glad to help.

I thought then that the whole matter had probably been blown out of all proportion. Too many former players were sounding off in the commentary box when they did not know a great deal about what was really going on. In due course Brian went back to first-class cricket for Trinidad and Tobago, as I always maintained he would. He said he needed to return to the game as much as he had wanted to escape from it at the end of the tour of England and we have to take him at his word. People suggested to me at the time that I should have been advising Brian, because I would understand better than anybody what he was going through. But the truth of the matter is that he was receiving the best advice from Wes Hall, his tour manager. Wes told him to be positive and not to be afraid of pressure.

In my view, Brian should be the *next* West Indies captain. He is a very good student of the game and has a first-class cricketing brain. His record of captaincy speaks for itself – captain of his secondary school, Fatima College; captain of the West Indies Schools team which toured Australia; captain of West Indies B team which toured Zimbabwe and captain of the Trinidad National team in the 1994 Red Stripe series.

Until the problems stemming from disagreements on the 1995 tour of England, the selectors, too, evidently saw him as a future leader, appointing him to be vice-captain on the 1994 tour of India. In addition to being an outstanding batsman and having a good cricketing brain, Lara has a quiet dignity which sets him apart as a natural cricketing ambassador.

CHAPTER 12

Captaincy

In my years as a player, Brian Close and Ian Chappell stood out as opposing captains. They, like Imran Khan, always played the game the way it should be played. They were always playing to win. Close was a very clear thinker on the game. He was never cowed by the reputation of any player and when a new batsman came to the crease he would crowd him. He understood that any batsman is most vulnerable in the early stage of his innings and he would apply maximum pressure and attack him in the area of any known weakness. No matter how good a batsman was, he would instruct his bowlers to get at him. I know. My reputation never bothered Close and he gave his bowlers the same instructions when I got to the crease.

I remember going in to bat at the Oval in 1966 and Close, who was leading England for the first time, crowding me. The wicket was very flat and I had made 81 in the first innings, but he told John Snow to give me a bouncer first ball. It did not get up. I swung too early, the ball hit the bottom edge onto my leg and there was Close standing at short leg with his eyes open to take the catch. I can think of no other fielder and no other captain who would have done that; he was one of a very special kind. Today's captains would do well to emulate him. He had courage, the basic quality for a good captain and any cricketer.

FOLLOWING THROUGH AT LORD'S IN HIS QUICKER STYLE. BOWLING
AGAINST ENGLAND IN 1966, WATCHED BY THE NON-STRIKER TOM
GRAVENEY

Ian Chappell was also a good captain. He was always looking for ways to win and was adept at spotting and exploiting his opponents' weaknesses. I believed in this attacking approach. I felt that any decision I made should put my team in a position to win. Too many captains, alas, try to make sure that they do not lose. I always thought that it was important to make the other side feel they had a chance of winning. If they did do so, then that would have been through playing decent cricket themselves and achieving a victory through a similarly positive approach. That is the way I like to see the game played.

Invincible attack

Clive Lloyd, the outstanding West Indies captain, was a very good leader of men who, by the sheer brilliance of his own performances, earned their respect and admiration. Undeterred by the fact that he lost his first series in Australia 5–1, he came up with the idea of a four-prong pace attack and developed the invincible attack of Croft, Holding, Roberts and Garner that took the world by storm. He had Sylvester Clarke and Wayne Daniel as back-ups. These two would have been front-line bowlers in any other Test team. When I tell today's players that Garner was the slowest of that lot but was very deadly on account of his great height and accuracy, they seem relieved that he, and all the others, are retired. At the time of writing, "Big Bird" – now in his 40s and greying – is still taking wickets in Barbados First Division cricket.

There are those who argue that because of the dominance of his fast bowlers, Lloyd had it easy as captain. I say the performance of each player inspired and reinforced the whole team's performance. The great thing about Lloyd was that he led by example whether batting, bowling or fielding. As a cover point in his youth, he was one of the greatest fielders I have seen and rates alongside the South Africans Colin Bland and Jonty Rhodes and the Australian Paul Sheahan.

Viv Richards did a marvellous job as West Indies captain. He, too, led by example. He did what he had to do and did it his way. His approach reminds me of Herman Griffith's famous words: "We all walk, but we all walk different." The important thing about Viv was that he got results – the record shows that he never lost a series. He was one of the greatest batsmen of all time. What particularly impressed me was that once the team was on the field, everybody knew who was captain.

Mixing the ages

There are times when a captain has to put his foot down and say and do things to assert his authority. It is always more difficult when dealing with a team of experienced players – some of whom may not be giving a hundred per cent on and off the field. Looking back, I can advise today's leaders that there is invariably more respect for the captain if there is a mix of youth and experience in the team.

On the other hand, if the captain himself is young, there may be problems. I sensed when Lara led Trinidad and Tobago in the 1992 Red Stripe tournament that because of his youth he did not always get total support from his players. He responded in typical fashion by completely dominating his team's batting performances, scoring 715 runs and passing Desmond Haynes's 654 in 1991 as the most runs scored by any batsman in the annual series.

Clive Lloyd understood very well that some of the more experienced players can be a handicap and stand in the way of building *esprit de corps*. He got rid of some of the older players and brought on board younger players hungry for cricket and keen to do well and keep their place on merit rather than on a fading reputation.

Allan Border, when he took over the captaincy of the Australian team, built a virtually new team. Critically, he had their respect as the senior player and did not retain too many from

140

his generation. People often repeat *ad nauseum* the facile axiom about having a team which is a blend of youth and experience, but many captains and former captains will confirm that the theory is often far better than the reality.

Insularity and island bias

Frankly, as far as the West Indies team is concerned, some of the current problems *may* stem from insularity. Lest we forget, the West Indies cricket team is a peculiar joint venture between players drawn from a number of different countries separated by thousands of square miles of water. Australia is one large country. So is India, and also England. An Australian is an Australian whether he plays for Western Australia or New South Wales and an Englishman is an Englishman whether he plays county cricket for Yorkshire or Middlesex.

But salt-water separation seems to breed insularity and I often get the impression that some of the players put national considerations above being, first and foremost, members of the West Indies team. Yet other people boast proudly that cricket is the predominant unifying force in West Indian life. Let me say now that in recent years I have seen evidence of insularity creeping back into West Indies cricket. Some of the curious selections that have been made suggest that the emphasis is more on appeasing particular insular interests than on putting together the best possible side. Let me warn the selectors, the players, the public and the numerous "experts" in the media – insularity and island bias pose a dangerous threat to the future of West Indies cricket and are self-defeating.

The burdens of captaincy

I am often asked by players, the media and the public whether being captain affects a player's performance. I say, not necessarily. It is the team which plays the major role. The burdens of captaincy are made easier to carry if the team plays together and everyone pulls his weight. We must always bear in mind that it is not possible for any cricketer to do it all on his own. Every player needs the help of the other ten men in the team. In a winning team every man is a winner.

Under Lloyd, the incentive of playing for significant financial rewards became an inducement for the highest level of performance. Whatever may have been the real or imagined stresses and problems among the players were put aside as the rewards which go with being world champions drew the players together. They were sufficiently shrewd not to let personal considerations get in the way of making money to secure their future.

No backward move

In my view, Brian Lara should be the next West Indies captain after Courtney Walsh. Richie Richardson had little option but to resign after the West Indies had been beaten by Kenya during the World Cup. It was not Richie's fault that he lost so many good players at once, but, alas, it seems that his tour parties were affected by ill discipline. Brian Lara is a very good student of the game and has a first-class cricketing brain. Richie Richardson, who had made a decent enough start in the job at a time when some commentators thought Desmond Haynes should have been appointed, seemingly no longer had the respect of the players, and before the World Cup various names were being suggested in the Caribbean to replace him. Among them was Courtney Walsh – which was a reasonable suggestion – and Roger Harper, who had played in only one Test match in eight years and who, rising 33, was past his best. It was a farcical idea.

West Indies cricket would have been going backwards had they appointed Roger as captain. The selectors should at this point have been building for the future and looking for a leader whose knowledge was respected. These different viewpoints did not help. In the old days, problems were to be expected because of the insularity among the islands. Now that all the players are professionals and well paid, there should be fewer difficulties. The fact that the rewards are so much greater should help to ensure that players stick together.

Yet it had reached the point after the West Indies elimination in the Benson and Hedges one-day series in Australia – remember, Sri Lanka got into the final, which would have been unthinkable in years gone by – at which their cricketers seemingly could not be fired. This would not have occurred in business. There was no player in that team other than Lara who was capable of making 50 or 60 in three consecutive innings. A batsman who made anything over 70 after four or five low scores would retain his place for the following year. The supporters were concerned about how the team was losing – that concern emanating from lack of faith in the captain. I would see the players hugging each other and doing the "high fives" on the field and think that there was no lack of team spirit. Then I would be amazed to hear there were problems between them.

Passing judgement

Aside from Lara pulling out of the trip to Australia, the selectors would have faced a further difficulty if they had appointed him captain. The West Indies were not known to sack their leaders. Rohan Kanhai was moved to one side in the mid-1970s and Gerry Alexander made way for Frank Worrell in 1960, playing under him without any sense of embarrassment to either of them. Otherwise, going right back to Frank, myself, Clive Lloyd and Viv Richards, such a possibility was precluded because the West Indies were generally a winning team. To be fair to Richie, he had to lead a number of experienced players, who might well have questioned his decisions when things went wrong. As was shown under Frank, it is far easier to take over a group of young players who will follow their leader without question or doubt. Frank – the best leader I ever played under – was the obvious choice at that time; his appointment was not questioned. If he had had to captain Jeff Stollmeyer, Everton Weekes and Clyde Walcott, it might have been a different matter, but no one else felt equipped to take over. Even if Frank had made mistakes, there was no one to pass judgement on him.

A *different style of leadership*

In his first stab at the captaincy Frank exploded the myth that a coloured man could not captain the West Indies successfully. He had a different style of leadership from what had hitherto been known in a colonial environment, which was "do so because I say so". He charmed, encouraged, led and corrected. He had a calming influence over excitable young players, among whom I was once numbered. His famous words to Wes Hall at a crucial stage of the Brisbane tied Test of 1960/61, with Australia needing a run to win off the last ball, are worth repeating here: "Remember, Wes, if you bowl a no-ball you won't be able to go back to Barbados." Poor Wes was so petrified that he bowled from behind the crease, somehow managing to retain his pace.

Many people have asked me since I retired why I decided to change my position in the batting order. The fact is, I didn't make the decision to go lower in the order at number six – Frank, my captain, decided that it was in the team's interest that I should bat at that position. It is, in fact, the place in the order where many all-rounders have traditionally gone in. As usual, Frank, astute reader of the game that he was, reasoned that my knowledge of the game put me in a position to follow it better and hence I could either attack or defend according to the circumstances at the particular time. In addition, Frank felt that I was more reliable under pressure.

Frank was not only a great captain but a great human being. I felt honoured to be named to succeed him as captain and, in a sense, to pick up the baton passed from him. He brought West Indies cricket together as an amalgam of all that is good in the West Indian personality.

The importance of luck

One of the problems inherent in judging a captain on the strength of results is that it is the players the captain has at his behest who make his reputation. Ian Chappell had some exceptional bowlers in Dennis Lillee and Jeff Thomson but primarily he had the full backing of his players because he possessed a young team who did not wish to show him up. Viv Richards was not given the credit he should have been as a captain, for he had to lead several older (and, for that matter, ageing) players. The exceptional captain who has not been lucky has yet to exist. They say that captaincy is 90 per cent luck and ten per cent skill, but don't try it without that ten per cent. As one who also had two outstanding fast bowlers at his disposal, namely Wes Hall and Charlie Griffith, I would concur with that. Leading the West Indies was altogether harder work after they had retired.

When Clive became captain in 1975, he, too, led a young team. The two remaining senior players, Rohan Kanhai and Lance Gibbs, did not last long. Hence, his task was all the easier, for there was no natural candidate to succeed him, even though he lost his first series in charge 5–1 to Australia in 1975–76. Also, he took over at a time when big money was flowing into the game, which, like it or not, does help players pull together. Personal differences are put aside when there are tangible rewards at stake. Success breeds contentment but you soon discover who is behind you when the team starts to lose. So

ON THE ATTACK FOR REST OF THE WORLD IN 1970

it would have made sense for a younger man to have taken over the captaincy at a time when Richie was clearly having problems in marshalling the older players. He could have started afresh and I would have been willing, and happy, to have assisted him in a managerial or coaching capacity.

Team management

I have never had any particular desire to manage a West Indies party on tour and consequently have turned down several invitations to do so. But if and when Brian becomes captain – or someone else who will most likely be young and inexperienced at captaincy – I would be happy to assist if required.

The one trip I did manage was that by the Holders Hill club in Barbados when they came to England in 1994. For a small village they have produced a large number of very good cricketers, including Desmond Haynes – whose Test career ended too abruptly and at too young an age. On this particular short tour, Holders Hill became the first village to play against MCC at Lord's, which was a thrilling occasion. They also played at Arundel and against Paul Getty's team on his own ground. I thoroughly enjoyed the experience but have had no ambition to try management even on an irregular basis.

Leading the West Indies

I am sometimes asked what sort of a captain Brian would make. I reply that it should be easier to lead professionals than amateurs because a professional should know his job and be able to give more input. The amateur, such as Frank and I included in our West Indies teams, might well have been a good cricketer but might also have asked why the game was being taken so seriously. One problem Brian or anybody else will face in the Caribbean is inter-island rivalry. The upshot of this is that more players want to be captain. Unlike the

CONGRATULATING BRIAN LARA AFTER HIS RECORD-BREAKING
INNINGS OF 375 AGAINST ENGLAND IN ANTIGUA

Australians, we tend to pick the captain first and then his team, a policy which seems to work for us. It is true that leading an XI containing four fast bowlers makes leadership simpler, for they can be rotated. Resting Joel Garner when there is Malcolm Marshall to take his place is every captain's dream.

Captaincy of the West Indies, however, no longer embraces that policy, for opposing batsmen have become accustomed to dealing with all-out pace and there are no longer bowlers of the calibre of Garner and Marshall to be called on. New Zealand even opened their attack with a spinner during the 1992 World Cup, a ploy that proved quite successful. Early in an innings batsmen are accustomed to playing themselves in and are accustomed to pace. Bowlers and captains have on occasion in the past been able to perform like robots. If Brian could withstand the exposure from television which highlights mistakes in field placing, then I believe he has the awareness and the authority to make for a highly competent captain of the West Indies. He obviously knows that it is a great honour to lead one's country on the field and understands the serious responsibilities this imposes off it. He clearly understands that in a very real way the captain of any national team in the West Indies is a sitting duck for the most perceptive and critical of all cricketing crowds in the world. I always felt when I was captain that I carried the full weight of all of the governments and peoples of these islands on my shoulders. It is an awesome responsibility.

CHAPTER 13

The Treadmill

The modern tour schedule takes a heavy toll on all the players, not just on a player who is as much in demand as Brian Lara is. While it is understandable that the cricket administrators want to fit in as much cricket as possible to attract as many paying spectators as they can, I believe that more consideration should be shown to the players, especially those on the visiting teams.

Take the 1994 West Indies tour of India. The visitors played eleven one-day games in 22 days. That is simply too demanding a regimen. In addition, they played a number of three-day matches and three Test matches which, in my opinion, were not sufficiently well scheduled.

These days, when the players have very vocal and articulate associations which put their case to the administrations, it would seem that they could argue for better-organized tour schedules. These would alleviate the need to travel long distances by train or air to play a particular match and then virtually retrace their steps to play another game the night after. No wonder the players often seemed jaded and uninterested, and anxious for the tour to end.

One of the things that have changed over the years is the quality of accommodation. It is very pleasing to all concerned that teams touring India now stay in the best hotels in Bombay,

Calcutta and New Delhi which in terms of facilities and service compare favourably with hotels anywhere in the world. Travelling with the team on occasion now as a commentator, I am in a good position to compare the facilities today with those in my day and I continue to be pleasantly surprised.

A problem traditionally faced by teams touring India has been food. Not everyone is accustomed to curry, a taste for which, for the uninitiated, can take some time to acquire – especially in the case of players who are accustomed to eating bland foods.

The English and Australian teams have got around this problem by taking along a chef and their own food and water, though bottled water is available everywhere now. West Indian teams touring India, Pakistan and Sri Lanka have never found it necessary to take their own chef or food. Hot, spicy food is part of normal Caribbean cuisine, and though there have been isolated problematical incidents, these days all types of cuisine are available in India.

Things were vastly different during my first tour to India in 1959 and during the 1966–67 tour. In those days, before leaving home it was a prerequisite to have a number of injections against contagious diseases, some of which caused an adverse reaction. These days it is only necessary to be inoculated against malaria since India has overcome many of the problems associated with under-development and is now a rapidly developing country.

Demanding schedule

But back to the frenetic schedule of tours which places tremendous physical and mental demands on players. The West Indies tour of India, which started in late October 1994, was the beginning of 12 months of non-stop cricket. When the tour finished in mid-December, they went to New Zealand to play two Tests and five one-day games before flying back home to play four Tests and three one-day games against the Aussies.

No sooner had that tour finished than they took off for England to play a record six Tests there, in addition to a heavy schedule of county and one-day matches. In less than one calendar year the West Indies played a staggering 15 Test matches. The cynics will say that it is the price to be paid for being at the pinnacle of world cricket for so long. That is true, of course, but let us not forget the heavy physical and mental demands of the game.

Too much cricket

It is my view that they have been called on to play too much cricket and only time will tell what effect this has on the players. Players cannot keep their fitness and appetite for the game after playing year-round. Though it is understandable that the New Zealand administration would have wanted the world's premier team out there for their centenary year's celebrations, in retrospect the West Indies Cricket Board may well wish to consider whether it was worth it.

Surely the players could have done with a period of rest and relaxation. The experience of Richie Richardson, the then West Indies captain, who had to stop playing county cricket for Yorkshire in 1994 and missed the Indian and New Zealand tours because of fatigue, should have sent a salutary message to the authorities. The same signal should have been picked up from the repeated furlough Brian Lara had to take from his county exertions at Warwickshire, flying home to Trinidad to get away from it all and recharge his batteries.

All countries are guilty of playing too much cricket. Too much cricket is worse than too little and results in staleness, loss of interest and lack-lustre performance. I see signs of fatigue and staleness among those who play county cricket and then go straight into a series of games on tour, leading to physical burn-out and mental tiredness, especially among the more seasoned players.

In the case of the West Indies, the authorities need to consider carefully the scheduling of tours to ensure that the Test players are available to play in the domestic Red Stripe series. This pits Barbados, Trinidad and Tobago, Jamaica, Guyana, the Leeward Islands and the Windward Islands against each other in four-day and one-day matches. The games allow the best young players to meet the Test stars and give spectators the opportunity to see the region's best players in action.

There is no greater school of learning and no greater fillip to success than seeing international icons in competition against each other. That is one of the great benefits of Red Stripe cricket each year. If you understand the very special relationship between West Indian representative teams and their followers – easily the most knowledgeable and most critical anywhere – then you will understand the mutually reinforcing need for each other.

The hectic schedule is part of the price the West Indies are now paying for their reputation as the game's most attractive team. All cricketing crowds want to savour the magic of Brian Lara's batting and the deadly accuracy and sheer pace of Curtly Ambrose. I suspect that rather than contracting, their schedule will expand, especially now that Sri Lanka and Zimbabwe are playing international fixtures and South Africa is back on the Test circuit. The West Indies Board, while not ignoring the financial benefits of having the world's most attractive team, must weigh carefully the adverse effects on the players of too much cricket and on the home crowds of depriving them of seeing their stars in action in domestic cricket.

County circuit or Leagues

Furthermore, the time is fast approaching when overseas players themselves must make critical decisions about whether it is to their overall benefit to play English county cricket. Now that the Test and County Cricket Board has placed further restrictions on overseas players, it would seem timely for the players themselves to contemplate their own future in county cricket. The question is, who benefits from playing cricket six and sometimes seven days a week over a five-month period? Taking on this intensive schedule, as I did in 1968, meant that I played an awful lot of cricket, but there were not so many tours, or indeed such intensive tours, at that time. There are so many weak counties that it is not difficult for a Test cricketer to collect easy runs. It seems to me that the best method of selection for Test cricket would be for the authorities to take heed of what we do in Barbados, which is to choose the best team from trials. Selectors do not go through a batsman's statistics and work out whether he made his centuries against good or bad opposition. They simply look at his average and enquire whether or not he is in good form.

How different the circuit is from the days when generation after generation of outstanding overseas cricketers played only one day a week – Saturday – in the Leagues in England. Overseas players might well ask themselves if it would not be better for them to seek such contracts. I have been impressed in recent years with the improved standard of the Leagues, which continue to attract overseas players who may be unable to make their own Test teams but would be good enough to play for some other countries. Indeed, although an overseas player would pick up, in the mid-1990s, £16,000 from a season of League cricket as opposed to around £30,000 from a county, he might find that if he were still playing Test cricket regularly, he would be better off in the long term. His career would be prolonged, especially if he were a fast bowler. The fact that the West Indies played 15 Test matches in ten months in 1994–95 means that their best players do not need to take part in county cricket to make a decent living. I would not have gone into it had I been making the sort of money Brian Lara has been making, for it is that much more tiring for an all-rounder than for a batsman. It should not be forgotten that the best batsmen in my early days, the three "W's" of Walcott, Weekes and Worrell, retained their standards during and after playing in the Leagues. In fact, several individuals who played at that level would remark that it was more arduous than county cricket.

Such cricket made me a better thinker and team man. I had to carry the team, whereas in county cricket every player is a professional, is paid and is consequently pulling their weight. The standard of pitches in the Leagues was not so good as in county cricket, so a batsman had to concentrate particularly hard. The pitches were not even covered overnight, although I submit that even if an uncovered pitch makes for a better technician, that is not a good enough reason for reverting to such a ruling in the first-class game. Given the amount of money paid to a pro and the fact that exposure to the elements might prevent any play the following day, pitches have to be properly protected from rain.

County and country

It might appear to some overseas players that they can make do without playing Test cricket, but that is not so. These days, unlike the 1960s when young cricketers such as John Shepherd and Keith Boyce were invited to join counties on account of their promise, a player is chosen to play county cricket because of his reputation. If he is out of Test cricket for a couple of years, he will be surprised by his county's reaction. And his reputation has to be forged against international opposition. Besides, I don't understand how some individuals can feel they would prefer to play for their counties than for their countries. If I had my way, those players would never be chosen for Test cricket again.

While it is true that playing in the Leagues is not as rewarding financially as playing on the county circuit, the physical wear and tear is significantly less. The ideal player for a League team is an all-rounder, and in recent years a number of bowlers who can bat and batsmen who can hold up an end have made their mark.

One thing I constantly drill into the heads of all cricketers is that they must remember at all times that Test cricket is still the summit of the game, and if a player is successful at the highest level there will be a clamour for his services at all other levels. While I acknowledge the pivotal place of one-day cricket as a crowd-puller and money-earner, for me the Test match is still the true measure of the world's best cricketers.

Another aspect of the game that has changed since I stopped playing is that there are not as many social events as before. For one thing, punishing travelling schedules severely erode the time for social events these days. In my day many a player who could not make the team made his mark on the social circuit. Some social events will always be mandatory, but all touring teams have cut back on the number they attend. Frankly, some social functions can be horribly tedious after a full day on the field. Yet we all need at some time to lighten up a bit, share a drink and a joke and talk about anything other than what took place on the field of play that day.

CHAPTER 14

Selection and Remuneration

One article that caught my eye recently included a comment from the South African fast bowler Fanie de Villiers that the financial rewards for leading Test cricketers were not commensurate with their achievements and their status as crowd-pullers. He said that cricketers are just as much performers as golf and tennis players are, and asked how it was that the golfer Ernie Els earned a hundred times what Jonty Rhodes, the brilliant young South African all-rounder, was earning. The South African Cricket Board obviously got the message, for the players were given a bonus of US$72,000 for impressive performances in their initial Test matches as well as for achieving victory in their one-day series against the one-day world champions, Pakistan.

The way forward

Cricketers deserve to be paid better. Golfers play for a purse which is invariably sponsored. In cricket, however, until a deal was worked out between the boards and a few large TV networks, funding was dependent primarily on gate receipts. In my view, the way forward for cricket could be sponsorship. Would it be unreasonable for the Boards of Control to ask five sponsors to put up, let us say, $100,000 each match for a series of five

Tests, with the winners getting $300,000 and the losers $200,000? Perhaps with all of the spin-off benefits to be derived from advertising, one sponsor may even wish to sponsor an entire Test series. When comparisons are made with golf, I have not heard any complaints, either from the sponsor or the players, about the very successful Johnny Walker tournaments.

When I remember what I was paid both as a Test player and as a county cricketer for Nottinghamshire, my mind boggles at the earnings of today's players. Let me hasten to add that most of them fully deserve what they earn. Brian Lara did enough for county cricket and the game globally in his year with Warwickshire to justify his huge earnings. Wherever he plays, sell-out crowds are guaranteed to keep the turnstiles busy following the club which, on account of his record-breaking achievements, won three out of the four major cricket tournaments in England in 1994.

All things considered, today's players are not badly taken care of financially. Their packages cover payment of bills for travelling, hotel expenses, meals, laundry, valet services and doctor's bills, leaving only personal telephone bills to be paid. Yet I am told that the players generally think they are inadequately compensated for what they contribute. They have their cogent arguments concerning the substantial amounts of money the game now attracts through sponsorship and television rights and how much of this actually spins off to them.

I was told when I played the game that I had made more money out of it than anyone before me. That may well have been true, although W G might have thought otherwise, but it was not a lot in comparison with the leading performers in other sports. It was certainly nothing compared with what top players receive today, even taking inflation into account. I was also disappointed by much of the financial advice and so-called guidance I was given in those days, although that is by-the-by. I became more wary and cynical about people who came up to me and proffered money-making schemes.

I lived well in my 20 years in the game, although the future began to concern me increasingly as I came towards the end of my career. But I don't feel envious about the earnings of players today. Of course, not all of them deserve to be so well paid. But in five years' time some of these same players might be envious of those who follow them and earn even more, because sport is not going to stand still. More money is constantly coming into cricket: every player now has a car, there is greater sponsorship than ever before, the facilities are more attractive and nearly every Test series is a sell-out. This all shows that the game is still very popular.

When people come up to me and say, "But, Gary, why do you not resent players of lesser ability than you making ten or 20 times what you did out of the game?" I just ignore them. The point is that in a different era I might have been doing different things. I might have been playing professional golf, football, basketball, table-tennis, tennis or wind-surfing. Who knows? Or I might not have played any sport for a living. Besides, what you have never had, you never miss. I've never run out of money because I've never really had any! I have never truly been very short of money.

Suitable rewards

I can't envisage financial rewards ever reverting to anything less than they are now. When I was playing, I couldn't imagine them being this high. The novelty of foreign travel and living in smart hotels was the compensation for youths from humble backgrounds such as myself. But, as a player grows older, this novelty soon wears off. The criterion is not playing for your country but the rewards you can achieve for so doing. There is a scale of pay and people expect commensurate rewards: even now, I still hear certain players complaining about the money they receive. It is sad the way the world has gone but this has to be accepted. This is not to say that there will not always be gaps

THE HOOK, PLAYED WITHOUT HAVING TO MOVE
FULLY FORWARD OR BACK

THE TRADEMARK HOOK, AND THIS ONE WENT FOR FOUR

between the earnings of a cricketer and those of a golfer or a footballer. For cricketers to read or hear that the footballer Tino Asprilla was joining Newcastle United in the English Premier league for wages of between £16,000 and £30,000 a week was mind-boggling. And that does not take account of his signing-on fee or transfer fee, which is how he makes much of his money. It is why a transfer system could come about in cricket.

The point is that there always was money in cricket. Those who sat in the boxes reaped the benefits; it kept the Boards of Control going and those whom they entertained. Certainly, little went back to the players. In the Caribbean the situation was complicated by only small sums of money coming through the gates. The grounds were not big enough and, although the authorities have tried to enlarge them, the requisite space is still not there. Besides which, the West Indian populace cannot afford to pay as much for their tickets as spectators elsewhere in the world. The price of a ticket for one day at Lord's is the equivalent of almost all five days of a Test in the West Indies. If it were not for the money coming into the Caribbean Boards through television, the players would not be nearly so well remunerated.

Honour or money

I supported World Series Cricket because I wanted to see the leading players earn more money from the game. I recall the letter I received from the West Indies Board of Control inviting me to join the party to tour England for the tour in 1963. In one sense, I would have played for my country for nothing, and yet the pay I was offered was depressing: it was not as much as I would have received for playing a season of League cricket with Radcliffe. What was more, I would be playing more cricket at a higher level and would have to undertake much more travel. This did not seem to be fair.

Wes Hall felt the same as I did. I spoke to Sir Donald Bradman and Richie Benaud, two of the most respected individuals in the game, and their unqualified advice was that I should go on the tour. What, they reasoned, if I did badly? Everybody would say that I wanted all this extra money and then I still failed the team. It was sound thinking. In those days there was a great deal of emphasis placed by administrators on the honour of representing one's country. They felt I would have had no sense of honour had I put financial rewards ahead of service to the West Indies. But it still took a letter from Frank Worrell to pull me round.

The youth question

Today, there is a natural nexus between what most cricketers earn and why they sometimes seem to loiter after closing time, as it were. The reason players now want to go on and on despite their increasing age, which can slow the reflexes, is the need to continue being high earners for as long as possible. Cricket is a game notoriously unkind to its stars when they hang up their boots, particularly in small societies with very limited employment opportunities. Similarly, the old pro in England is not likely to earn more than a moderate wage. In the Caribbean of the 1950s, administrators sometimes gave the impression that once a cricketer's career was over, he could quietly be forgotten. They did not concern themselves with what the future held – or did not hold – for him.

Yet I think that, too often, some selectors, in their unseemly haste to bring young players into their teams, not only behave in an unkind and insensitive manner but also make basic selection mistakes. There can be no doubt that the West Indies selectors invested too heavily in young and unproven players in the 1992 World Cup in Australia. In the process they squandered the opportunity to select the best available team.

Gordon Greenidge and Viv Richards, then still two of the most dominant batsmen in world cricket and capable of taking any bowling attack apart, should have played in the World Cup. The prospect of having Viv coming to the crease at number five or six would have filled any opposing team with despair, even if by then he was in his sunset years. Perception in cricket, like in so much else in life, can often be as daunting as reality, and both Gordon and Viv were awesome psychological weapons in the West Indies arsenal.

It was a terrible pity that two of the greatest of all West Indian batsmen were sacrificed on the altar of the insistent urge to bring young players into the team while tried and proven ones still had something to contribute. Obviously, nobody should knock the efforts to bring young players of merit on board, but they must earn their place. By all means give youth a chance but let them merit selection. Yet it works both ways: England clearly were mistaken in taking Graham Gooch and Mike Gatting to Australia in the 1994–95 series when they were obviously well past their best.

My philosophy from my early years in the West Indies team when playing alongside revered players like Weekes, Walcott, Worrell, Ramadhin and Valentine was that if youth is good enough it will always come to the fore. That was how my generation of players – Hunte, Kanhai, Nurse, Hall, Griffith and Gibbs – forced their way into the team. If a player has youth and talent on his side, what else can he want? A little luck, perhaps: that always helps, no matter what else one has going.

Franklyn Stephenson

The player who I continue to think was really hard done by because he was always deemed "too old" is Franklyn Stephenson, the Barbados, Nottinghamshire and Sussex all-rounder. In his heyday he was a really outstanding all-rounder, yet he was continually bypassed for selection by the West Indies. I wonder what grievous sin he committed or which important person he offended. If it was because he went to South Africa with a "rebel team", he should have been forgiven eventually. He was still left in the wilderness of despair when players of inferior ability were commanding regular places in the team.

Stephenson's ability to bat, bowl and field to a very high level of proficiency distinguished him as the best all-round cricketer the West Indies has produced in the last 15 or 20 years. He was my natural successor but never got the opportunity to play regularly for Barbados or even once for the West Indies. As if to cock a snook at the selectors, Franklyn did the "double" when he replaced Richard Hadlee as Nottinghamshire's all-rounder in 1988. To take 100 wickets and score 1000 runs in his first season of county cricket was a tremendous achievement.

Here is a case of a player who was dominating the game in South Africa and on the English county scene, when he was considered by the powers that be to be well past his best, and who was persistently ignored by the selectors. This is an outstanding example of how the West Indies selectors cold-shouldered a player of considerable all-round ability at a time when he was precisely what the team needed to give it perfect balance. He will end his days as an active player wondering whether there was something other than abundant cricketing skill that the selectors were looking for. Franklyn Stephenson would easily have walked into any other Test team in the world and covered himself in glory. Yet he was never honoured with the greatest accolade any West Indian player can aspire to – a maroon West Indies Test cap.

CHAPTER 15

Claims and Counter-
claims

One of the greatest traumas to have occurred within the game in recent times has been the epidemic of allegations by cricketers against both their contemporaries and ex-players about match-fixing, and the intrusion of bookmakers taking substantial illegal bets on the outcome of matches. When I heard early in 1995 that members of the Pakistan team who went to South Africa had been made to swear on the Koran that they would not deliberately lose a game or accept bribes, I started to wonder aloud what had gone wrong with this noble game.

There have been rumours of bribe-taking and throwing matches for some time since I retired from the game. I recall that during the 1979–80 Pakistan tour of India, it was said that large sums were bet on one match and the bookmakers took such heavy losses that they declared all the bets null and void. There were also rumours about match-fixing when Pakistan, who were the overwhelming favourites, lost to Australia in the semi-finals of the 1987 World Cup in Lahore. Rumours were rife during the one-day series in Sharjah in 1990–91, too.

As far as I know, nothing ever came of these rumours and until recently neither the players nor the cricket administrations seemed concerned. Now the cricketing world is in shock over allegations and claims and counter-claims involving the names of some of the best-known players and ex-players.

It is a serious challenge to the integrity of the players and the game. These scandals are another aspect of the changing face of cricket which attracts public attention for all the wrong reasons. If any allegations are proven to be true, it will drag the game into disrepute.

Undermining the game

To hear Sarfraz Nawaz, the fast bowler turned politician, allege that the one-day international between England and Pakistan at Trent Bridge in 1992 was fixed seems incredible. His further claim that that was just one of the games that were fixed over 14 years involving his native Pakistan is very bothersome. He also talks of phone-tapping by the Pakistan Secret Service, an investigation of players' bank accounts and the government gathering evidence of bribery and match fixing with possible legal prosecution to follow. This is the stuff of which good novels can be written but is it the reality of international cricket at the end of what has been one of the game's most glorious periods?

All of this is very bad for Pakistan and worse still for cricket wherever it is played. Every effort must be made to get to the bottom of what is clearly an emerging problem that could undermine the game's integrity and ruin the reputations of some of its leading personalities. As to the penalties for those found guilty, I was pleased to see that Imran Khan denied that he had recommended hanging as a suitable penalty for those found guilty. Surely to take a human life in such circumstances would be an exaggerated penalty for the crime committed. The onus should be on each cricket-playing country to punish any deliquent player by banning him from playing for life and even banning him from attending major games, in the same manner that in horse-racing those guilty of breaking the rules are "warned off".

The ICC should ensure that the severity of the punishment fits the crime and lay down adequate penalties for each

Board to impose on delinquent players. If for any reason the national Board of any country refuses to carry out the recommended sanctions, then that country should be expelled from the ICC. Countries and cricketers must remain loyal to a code of conduct which outlaws any behaviour that will bring the game into disrepute.

My own experiences

Daily, I am asked if I was ever approached with a bribe to fix a match. I always say that bookmakers and match-fixers know whom to approach and would never have dared to approach me. Those who have been approached either in the recent past or before then must have given some hint that they were willing to do a deal. There is no one who was ever acquainted with me who could claim that they ever saw any indication that I would be susceptible to match-fixing or bribe-taking. Indeed, looking back on two decades of active cricket, I cannot recall having done anything to bring the game into disrepute or invite public opprobrium.

But I go further. Cricket is a team sport and the whole team shares responsibilities individually and severally, to a greater extent than in most other games. It would therefore mean that all 11 players would have to go along willingly, without protest and without disagreement, with a ploy to accept a bribe to fix a match. It is unthinkable that in any of the teams in which I played anyone could have attempted to offer a bribe to a player and not feel the weight of our collective fury. Football may be different in that a goal-keeper may deliberately let a goal slip through. But in cricket if a wicket-keeper was seen to be deliberately letting through byes or dropping catches, he would soon be removed and reviled as a traitor. In any case, bearing in mind the substantial salaries modern-day cricketers earn, only a very stupid player would put his career and his future on the line by being involved in nefarious activities on and off the field.

The only betting with which I and the West Indian players of my generation were familiar was the occasional flutter on the horses. A number of my contemporaries used to enjoy a wager, especially on the big races such as the Guineas, Oaks and the Derby. Wes Hall and I were the best-known punters and we went on to buy and race a few horses of our own. In our playing days we had friends who were owners, trainers and jockeys and we always managed to obtain information from these sources.

Part of the fun for us was not only in taking on the bookies but also in taking on the English players. They, too, had their sources of information and we enjoyed trading tips and seeing who could beat the bookies. It was all great fun and did much to relieve the boredom of playing cricket day in and day out. At times it was also quite profitable and I still have little mementoes – tie clips, cufflinks and so on – bought out of winnings. I am sure that if there had been various lotteries around in our time, most of the players would have tried their luck.

Let me also say that when we played in the larger countries like Australia and India and when we spent much time travelling great distances by train or in England by coach, the team would play three-hand brag, bridge or rummy as we moved from one destination to the other. It kept everyone occupied and helped to pass the time. If any wagers were exchanged, they were always small.

Recent allegations

On a personal level, I was stunned to hear allegations about Mushtaq Mohammad. I know him well. I played with him for both the Cavaliers and the Rest of the World teams and against him for West Indies and on the county circuit. I have always held him in the highest esteem both as a player and a man. I am therefore alarmed to read allegations that he is said to have approached Allan Border at Edgbaston in 1993 to throw the

Test between England and Australia. My friend Mushtaq is now reported as saying in the press that he was speaking with Border in jest. This entire episode is bizarre and bewildering, and it cries out for an investigation that will get to the root of the matter.

One thing that must concern all cricket lovers is that some of the biggest names in Pakistan and Australian cricket of the modern age are being bandied about as being allegedly involved in cricket's potentially nastiest scandal. Can these players – Border, Mushtaq, Salim Malik, Mark Waugh, Shane Warne and Tim May – give of their best with such allegations, rumours and counter-rumours regarding match-fixing and bribes? Justice must be done and must be seen to be done expeditiously in the interest of all.

It was alleged that Salim, when he captained Pakistan against Australia in 1994, attempted to fix matches by persuading his opponents to play badly, offering great sums of money by way of reward. Warne and May, the two spin bowlers who would have important roles to play on dry pitches, said that they were offered $200,000 – whether this was each or between them was not made clear – to bowl badly on the crucial final day of the first Test. Waugh has also said he was approached by Salim and asked for Australia to arrange to lose a one-day match. When challenged over this, he said simply, "Why should I want to make this up?" The alleged bribes were rejected and, in fact, Australia lost both matches.

After the players returned home, officials took statements from them which were sent to the International Cricket Council. What was peculiar was that neither Australia nor the ICC informed Pakistan about the accusations. The captain of a country had been charged with trying to fix matches and his employers had not been informed of it. Inevitably the Pakistanis were furious and when the story leaked out to an Australian newspaper, long after the event, everybody looked culpable through not having acted swiftly and decisively. Everybody,

that is, apart from Sir Clyde Walcott. Having seen the dissatis-
faction caused when the Pakistanis conducted an internal
inquiry and found Salim and everybody else to be blameless,
he asked the ICC member countries for the power to look into
the matter. He is a man of the utmost integrity and would auto-
matically command respect.

The Australian Board naturally defended their own players, but that was also tantamount to saying Salim really had
offered bribes. The Board had refused to send its players to
Pakistan to testify to the authorities there, reasoning that they
might be in danger and, anyway, had nothing to add to their
statements. It was all a dreadful way to carry on and smacked of
continuing bitterness between the two countries, their acri-
mony having carried over since the tour led by Allan Border
seven years earlier had ended in aggravation. The desire to
restore good relations seemed to override any thoughts of
trying to ascertain who was right and who was wrong in an
affair that harmed the game considerably more than any individual. When Salim joined the Pakistanis in Australia for their
tour in 1995, he inevitably did not contribute much. His colleagues were embarrassed by his presence and the Australians
ignored him. Fortunately the two captains, Mark Taylor and
Wasim Akram, hit it off to an extent that the series passed without any unpleasantness.

Negative influences

Before the first Test on the Pakistanis' 1992–93 tour, four players were arrested on a beach and charged with possessing
marijuana. The charges were dropped but the players wanted
the remainder of the tour called off, stating that they did not
have the mental or physical commitment to continue. Not
surprisingly, Pakistan were well beaten in the three-match
series. What with that and the accusations of bribery and
ball-tampering (see Chapter 9), they are attracting a lot of

opprobrium. I am amazed at what is happening to them and that a strong team has fallen apart so suddenly. I have to admit that I just do not understand it all and can only speculate to what extent the money in the game has affected them. In my day, the likes of Hanif Mohammad and Saeed Ahmed always seemed to be on top of everything.

Drugs, I am glad to say, did not affect the game or any of the players in my day. I know of no player who took drugs. Indeed, the first I heard about this afflicting the game was when accusations were levelled against English players in New Zealand in 1983–84. A sequence of newspaper stories culminated in some extraordinary allegations. Ian Botham was named in connection with drugs parties, one of which was supposed to have taken place in the dressing-room while England were being beaten by New Zealand in the second Test. I was relieved to see that all these allegations came to nothing.

CHAPTER 16

Remaining in the Game

During my time as a player, commentating on television and on radio as well as reporting in daily newspapers was largely undertaken by professional journalists. Some former cricketers chose to join the media, but they were few and far between. Richie Benaud had trained as a news and court reporter in his youth in Australia and hence became practised at his craft. Others, such as Denis Compton, were assisted by "ghosts", sports writers who played a key role in putting their thoughts into words. I was never of the opinion that a cricket critic had to have played the game at the highest level in order to be able to pass judgement on my performances and yet now the press boxes and commentary positions are filled with former cricketers, regardless of their standing in the game.

Broadcasting and writing

When I retired from first-class cricket, I never considered a career in broadcasting or writing. For one thing, I was not a good watcher of the game when I was not in the middle. I always remember Sir Frank Worrell, the greatest of West Indian captains and a man who shaped my life in numerous ways, saying that if we spent too long on the dressing-room balcony when our side were batting, the opposition's bowlers would believe they were better than they really were. This is not to say that attitudes elsewhere have corresponded with my viewpoint. Geoffrey Boycott was a cricketer I greatly admired. His belief when he was leading his county and country was that he should watch each and every ball intently. The young players in his team would, he reckoned, expect him to do so. But then Geoff was a very different person and cricketer to me: he was far more intense and was, in effect, a self-made person and batsman. We in the Caribbean are more spontaneous. I could cat-nap in the pavilion and wake up shortly before going out to bat: I do not believe Geoff would ever have done that. There is a danger, though, of a batsman who is waiting his turn to go in becoming too tense and wound up over what he has to do when he goes out to the middle.

I knew that sitting behind a microphone at a ground for six or seven hours a day was not for me. Commentating, if it was going to be done properly, needed to be worked at properly. I did not wish to undertake the travelling that was involved and, besides, I was bitten by the golf bug at the time. If I was going to take it seriously, I would have had to begin as soon as I finished my career. And there were no satellite television companies offering huge sums to former players, as is the case today. The media in Barbados – and in the Caribbean generally – was restricted. Any role I could have undertaken, unless it involved studio work, would have been strictly part-time. And after years of earning my living out of doors, I was not one to be constricted by staying inside.

The coverage of cricket has increased in accordance with the extra cricket played now. There are more tours, Tests and one-day internationals, hence there are more journalists. Press conferences are therefore a good idea. I feel relationships between press and players have improved accordingly. Do not imagine that the problems players have now with tabloid reporters seeking their own angles and story-lines is a new development. When I led West Indies, I was constantly caught up with having to fend off questions about Charlie Griffith's action. I was fortunate enough to have Jeffrey Stollmeyer, another former West Indies captain, as my manager on the 1966 tour of England. The tact and diplomatic skills he demonstrated were very apparent throughout, for there were snide remarks about Charlie which left a nasty taste in the mouth. I don't think any cricketer was pushed so deep into the freeze since Harold Larwood during the bodyline affair before I was born.

No West Indian touring team had had a more hostile reception from the press, which included ex-players who should have known better. Some members of the public gave us a hard time, too. I could see these people coming, at parties, receptions, hotel lounges, in the street. First, the big smile. Next, the slap on the back. The gush of praise, the overdose of flattery. I always knew what was coming next. They did not want to know about cricket – they wanted dirt. I felt that, rather than coming to me, they ought to go round some seedy book shops, where they would be able to buy plenty of it. As a captain, I required the nerve of a gambler, the poise of a financier, the human understanding of a psychologist, ten years' more cricket knowledge than I could ever possess, and the patience of a saint. I like to think I had a good relationship with the press. I read E W Swanton regularly and appreciated that he was the most impartial and authoritative of critics. There were plenty of other fine, informed correspondents whom I read, but I had no desire to join their number.

Umpiring

I took the same view of umpiring, which involves an even closer scrutiny of the game than does commentating. Now that there is a need for a third umpire and a match referee in Test cricket – both based in the pavilion, and the umpire with the benefit of a television monitor – more top players will be attracted than before. The International Cricket Council decided that these roles, as well as the introduction of so-called neutral umpires, were necessary at the very highest level. Years ago I advocated a panel of Test umpires selected by the captains of every country. If these proved to be not up to the job, then they could be dropped and replaced. I thought this would be a better idea than a panel of neutral umpires, but nothing came of my proposal. It is sad that times have changed – I never queried an umpire's decision in my career, but the large sums of money that have come into the game have, alas, had a telling effect. Standards of behaviour have deteriorated. So there are now opportunities for former stars such as Everton Weekes and Clive Lloyd, who would understandably rather remain in the pavilion than stand outside in all types of weather for long periods.

Administration

I never considered becoming an administrator within the game after I retired. An indoor existence was never going to be the life for me and I would have been particularly irked at the slow pace at which committees moved. Most successful administrators had to be political animals, embracing a certain diplomacy at which Englishmen are notably adept. I remember that when Imran Khan attended a sub-committee meeting of the International Cricket Council at Lord's, shortly after he himself had retired, he could not come to terms with the amount of lobbying done by delegates from member countries when the meeting was adjourned. It is not an easy game unless you are inclined that way, are prepared to tolerate endless paperwork and telephone calls and, if not remunerated or paid anything other than expenses, are preferably either retired or of independent means. You can put in a quarter of a century's work, as Peter Short has done both with Barbados and the West Indies Board, and yet still gain little thanks or recognition.

You are not noticed when the team is winning and you are criticized when it is losing. Peter had a very difficult year following Australia's victory over the West Indies in the Caribbean and was not inclined to stand for office again when his term as President expired in 1996. He also had to cope with political shenanigans between the islands which resulted in the administrative departments of the Board of Control moving from Barbados to Antigua. I admire the likes of Peter May and Colin Cowdrey for putting a great deal back into the game through giving their services free of charge as administrators, committee members or selectors, but I fear it was to the detriment of their health. Both the media and the public are increasingly demanding.

On the other hand, an administrator's job does offer a security which is not given to the captain. A man such as Colin can exercise power at MCC, the ICC, his county, Kent, and his nearest cricket club and ground, Arundel, without having the presidency or chairmanship taken away from him in the manner that the captaincy was when he was leading England. The members of a club can theoretically take an administrator or treasurer to task and the officers of a Board of Control can make life difficult for the secretary or chief executive. Occasionally, this happens. Most of the time, though, it is apparent that this is a job for the full term of office, if not for life.

Other forms of involvement

So, if I was not going to commentate or officiate, how else could I remain in the game? I have often been asked to undertake speaking engagements or to present prizes and man-of-the-match awards. There is a demand now for after-dinner speakers which, again, was not so prevalent when I was a player. It is possible to make a very good living by giving a talk at one or two dinners a week, but you have to be very fluent to do so. I remember presenting BBC Television's Sports

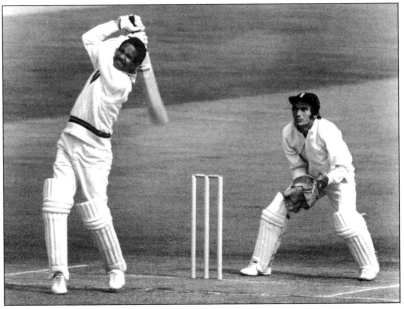

THE SOBERS SWING IS REMARKABLY SIMILAR IN BOTH HIS
FAVOURITE SPORTS

Personality award to Daley Thompson, that fine athlete, after I had retired. In those circumstances you are required to say only a few words and it is all too easy to sound trite. On this occasion Daley was overcome by nerves in a way he would never have been on the track.

I am happiest taking part in a cricket forum around a table or being interviewed on radio or television. The advent of one-day internationals inevitably meant that there was more opportunity for me to be a match adjudicator. The role of a cricket manager, at home or abroad, is not a new one; neither, for that matter, is that of a delegate at ICC meetings. I was always happy to give my opinion and was pleased to be asked, but committees can be long, tedious affairs. And I am not a politician.

Two Tributes

Citation given by Professor Henry Fraser, Public Orator of the University of the West Indies when the university conferred on Sir Gary an Honorary Doctorate of Laws at the Barbados campus in 1992:

Mr Chancellor, I present to you the man who has done more than anyone else in 365 years of recorded history, to bring Barbados to the attention of the rest of the world. Garfield St Auburn Sobers was born on 28 July 1936 in the Bay Land, St Michael. He was the last but one of seven children of Showmont and Thelma Sobers.

His father was a merchant seaman, away from home for long spells at a time, and he died when the young Garfield was only six. But the strong discipline, family unity and parental influence of the household had their effect, as every good parent knows, early in life.

By the age of eight, Gary with his brothers was busy organizing local cricket with home-made bat, ball and stumps, and arranging tournaments between the boys of the neighbouring villages. They played on the outfield of the Bay pasture, the early home of the Wanderers Cricket Ground arena of the great Harold Austin and George Challenor.

Garfield was in great demand in the Wanderers' nets, especially for his spin bowling, but even as a youngster he could bowl fast or slow as the occasion demanded. The national team of Bay Land thought him too small for competition, and his talents were spotted by a family friend, Garnet Ashby, the "strong man" showman of the '40s and '50s.

Garnet garnered him at age 15 to his BCL country team of Penny Hole, St Philip, a rustic seaside village now modernized and renamed Gemswick. What is not generally known is that Gary was once, briefly, a budding musician. The story goes that at age 14 he was spotted by Captain Wilfred Farmer, who had him recruited into the Police Band.

He then moved, via the Police Boys' Club, into the Police Sports Club so that he could play for the Police team. After only two years of club cricket, he represented Barbados against India in February 1953 as a spin bowler, taking seven wickets and bowling 40 maiden overs in the match.

In 1954, at 17, he played his first Test. He replaced Valentine in the last Test against England at Sabina Park, as a spin bowler. He took four wickets and scored 40 runs, but his arrival signalled the start of an era, the Sobers era, of both West Indian cricket and world cricket.

Greatness can be gauged in many ways, and the record books will detail Sir Garfield's extraordinary career for many years. Let us begin with the record of the highest Test innings of all time – 365 runs. The numerologists will have noted that 365 is also the number of years since the Afro-European settlement of Barbados in 1627.

But to continue: 93 Test appearances, the highest aggregate of runs in Test matches at the time of his retirement, exceeded since only by batsmen playing many more innings, together with 109 catches and 235 wickets, not to mention "impossible" feats such as hitting six sixes in one over.

But no mere schoolboy cricketer and ignoramus like myself has the right to comment on Sir Garfield's achievements. I prefer to borrow from the eloquent testimony of the recognized scholars of the game. The great, late C L R James wrote, "Sobers was the greatest of living batsmen." John Arlott, doyen of cricket writers, described him as the finest all-round player in the history of cricket. And our own Caribbean renaissance man and craftsman of language, Michael Manley, wrote in his History of West Indies Cricket: "He was so great a player that one must be careful lest he obscure the history of events and the texture of the times." And again: "Sobers was destined, in typically Caribbean fashion, to shine like some great star alone in the firmament of his own genius."

It is characteristic of his modesty that Gary Sobers should have written in his first book, Cricket Advance!, *in 1965 that "comparison with Bradman is one of the worst fates that can befall any cricketer". Bradman himself in the foreword to that book wrote, "Sobers's record entitles him to be ranked with the world's great batsmen."*

In fact, when seven years later, at Melbourne in 1972, Sobers scored 254 flawless runs in 376 minutes, Sir Donald said: "I believe Gary Sobers's innings was probably the best ever seen in Australia."

He proceeded to make a remarkable film analysing Sobers's batting, and made no bones in saying that he was describing a genius.

His bowling has been summarized by the Barbadian cricket writing triumvirate, Sir Carlisle Burton, Ronnie Hughes and Professor Keith Sandiford, in the recent book 100 Years of Organized Cricket in Barbados, 1892 to 1992 *in this way: "He became in fact the complete bowler. No individual in the history of cricket has been as versatile a bowler as Sobers at his peak."*

But it was his fielding which perhaps best expressed the sheer beauty of the natural athlete and the dramatic qualities of movement in cricket. Here again is Manley on Sir Garfield's first Test match: "In the first over Hutton steered a ball from Frank King in his general direction. Sobers moved to his right, picked up, half-pivoted, being a left-hander, and returned the ball like a bullet to the wicket-keeper. The whole thing was done with a feline quality; with that fluidity that is the hallmark of the athlete who goes beyond skill into some other extraordinary realms of unconscious co-ordination."

Sobers had arrived.

And Arlott, in his Book of Cricketers, *writes: "Everything he did was marked by a natural grace, apparent at first sight. When he walked out to bat, six feet tall, lithe but with adequately wide shoulders, he moved with long strides which, even when he was hurrying, had an air of laziness, the hip joints rippling like those of a great cat."*

On that note we must return to the words of the prophet and scribe of West Indies cricket, history, life, literature and art, C L R James himself. He answers the question "What is art?" himself, in his textbook of Caribbean life and culture, Beyond a Boundary: *"Cricket," he says, "is first and foremost a dramatic spectacle. It belongs with the theatre, ballet, opera and the dance."*

He concedes: "It cannot express the emotions of an age on the nature of the last judgement . . . It must repeat. But what it repeats is the original stuff of which everything visually or otherwise artistic is queried. The popular democracy of Greece, sitting for days in the sun watching The Oresteia; the popular democracy of our day, sitting similarly, watching Miller and Lindwall bowl to Hutton and Compton – each in its way grasps at a more complete human existence."

Sir Garfield Sobers is not only the greatest cricketer in the world, he is the embodiment of the West Indian dream. To quote Burton, Hughes and Sandiford again: "As an international star lifting himself to the top by the magnificence of his cricket, Sobers has served as a role model to thousands of lower-income Barbadian boys. He has been the role model also for millions of youngsters beyond the shores of Barbados. He is the single most popular of all Barbadians and he has taken our name to all parts of the world and covered it with glory."

Sir Garfield lacks the one all too common characteristic of so many great and popular international stars – conceit. His modesty is disarming. His generosity of heart, his spontaneity, and his willingness to help whoever he can remain unspoilt by unrivalled adulation – more than anyone in cricket history except possibly Bradman.

His versatility made him a national footballer and basketballer in his teens, and in more recent years, a national golfer. His desire to do well and to see his team do well in every endeavour combined with a rare ability to concentrate on the task in hand, to apply himself to the task, and to enjoy every minute of it. He continues to inspire, in word as well as deed, speaking to local clubs and groups, and working as a consultant for the Ministry of Tourism, promoting Barbados as a sports tourism destination.

He has liaised with over 200 cricket teams coming to Barbados, while the Sir Garfield Sobers International Schools Tournament has become a major event over the last six years. Like Sir Frank Worrell, his mentor and friend, Sir Garfield Sobers has become a hero in his own lifetime. His impact has gone far beyond the boundary, and it is timely that the University of the West Indies should recognize this.

That it should do so in the 365th year of our history, is but par for the Sobers course and the perfect Sobers timing. Mr Chancellor, I *have the greatest pleasure in calling on you to receive into the fellowship of the University of the West Indies, an artist and athlete supreme, a West Indian hero and a hero of the world, Sir Garfield Sobers, with the degree of Doctor of Laws honoris causa.*

*　*　*

Remarks made by the Prime Minister of Barbados, Hon. Owen Arthur, in November 1994 at the launch of the book *An Area of Conquest: Popular Democracy and West Indies Cricket Supremacy*, edited by Professor Hilary Beckles:

The Duke of Wellington said that the battle of Waterloo was won on the playing fields of Eton. I believe that the struggle for the emancipation of the people of the British West Indies and the full flowering of their creative talents, national pride and self-esteem won significant gains on the cricketing fields of the world. In an all-conquering constellation of stars none shone brighter than Sir Gary.

The tributes paid to him over the last four decades testify adequately to his bench-mark genius as the greatest cricketer ever. In everything he did on and off the field, he seemed to be pursuing a personal vision as a man driven by unique genius, the likes of which the world may never see again. In recent times, Sir Gary's unparalleled understanding of the technical aspects of the game has enhanced radio commentaries across the Caribbean and beyond. By common agreement among his colleagues and the listening public, Sobers in the box, like Sobers on the field, stands that much taller than the others.

He has always been the peerless exemplar of cricketing excellence. The trademark upturned collar, the lissome walk which defies emulation, the natural charm and quiet dignity, inspired my generation of Barbadian schoolboys to say, "I want to be like him when I grow up." It became a triumph of hope over experience but we treasure the inspiration.

In an era which saw contemporary international icons unique in their fields like Muhammad Ali and Pele, it is quite impossible to measure the sense of pride which we as a people felt in knowing that a Barbadian colossus who rose from the poverty of the Bay Land stood

183

alongside them at the pinnacle of international achievement and acclaim.

Sir Gary, with great humility but unbridled pride and joy, I salute you for your genius, your humility, your dignity, your fellowship and your sportsmanship. We give thanks to God that you were born on this 21 by 14 rock. We thank you for conquering the world and leaving your signature indelibly on the game wherever it is played. We thank you for retiring among us to inspire today's youth in their search for excellence.